2022 Edition

Life in the UK Test

Practice Questions and Answers

Edited by Lewis Sweeney

You can access 100s of free test questions on our website liveintheuk.co.uk. You will also find our 2022 British citizenship course which covers all of the content and what you need to learn in order to pass the Life in the UK test.

Use discount/access code: LIFEINTHEUKQA

ISBN: 9798412009025 (print)

Republished in the UK by Live in The UK Publishing

Table of Contents

Introduction to the 2022 edition

In this 2022 edition of 'Life in the UK Test: Questions & Answers' you will find 17 practice tests with over 400 updated questions from over 100 topics. All of the questions in this Question and Answer book are basked on the Life in the UK: A Handbook for New Residents issued by the Home Office. You will be quizzed on all aspects of British life including the culture, history and traditions of the UK stretching back over 1000 years.

The questions are all multiple choice and come in a number of types. Some questions have 4 possible answers and you need to **select one option** A, B, C or D. For example:

Which date is boxing day?

  A. 25th of December Each Year

  B. **26th of December Each Year**

  C. 27th December Each Year

  D. 29th December Each Year

Or you will be given a statement and asked whether it is is **TRUE** or **False**, for example:

Alfred Hitchcock was a famous film director?

Other questions will ask you to **select two** options:

Which are the two houses of parliament?

A. The House of Lords

B. The House of Commons

C. The House of Windsor

D. The House of Representatives

The answers are towards the back of the book and include an explanation of the correct answer. You can use these to identify areas you need further study in. Where there is the option for two answers you must get both right in order to get the point for that question. Overall you must get at least 18 out of 24 questions correct in order to pass. That means there is a passing threshold of 75%.

You will have 45 minutes to answer all the questions. Remember this is a multiple choice test so if you are not sure at first simply move onto the next question and come back to it at the end. Ensure you read the questions throughly and the you understand exactly what the question is asking.

What could come up?

The mock questions in this book cover key aspects of British life, culture and identity which may come up during the official test. The handbook has 5 chapters that you are expected to have a complete command of:

The values and principles of the UK

Democracy – the course covers all the fundamentals of the UK political system including elections, parliament and local authorities.

The rule of law - understanding the British legal system including civil, criminal and public law.

Individual liberty - your rights and freedoms as a British citizen.

Tolerance of those with different faiths or beliefs - understanding the multi-cultural nature of British life and the diverse collection of cultures and customs that make up the UK.

Participation in community life - making your own contribution to the community

What is the UK?

Understanding the geography of the four countries the UK is comprised of; Scotland, England, Wales and Northern Ireland.

A long and illustrious history

The history of the UK from its foundations through the Middle Ages, rise as a global power and 1945 onwards. Royal history including the Tudors, Stewarts, Elizabeth I, James VI and the English Republic ruled over by Oliver Cromwell.

A modern, thriving society

Understanding life in the UK today, the diverse religions customs and traditions that are practiced in the UK. The places of interest, arts and culture that are distinctively British and are a key part of British identity.

The UK Government, the law and your role

The British constitution and the role of parliament, the monarchy and key governmental institutions. Your rights and responsibilities under the law and the fundamental principles underpinning them.

How do I book a test?

There are around 30 test centres all around the UK and you can book your test on the .gov website. Each test costs £50 and there are evening and weekend slots available at many of the test centres.

How do I learn the content to pass the test?

There's more free tests on our website **liveintheuk.co.uk** and we also have courses on British citizenship that will help prepare you for the official test. The 100% online course is designed to breakdown the Life in the UK handbook down onto small bitesize lessons. You can also access the content on the go as the learning platform is mobile optimised.

You can track your progress throughout the course through your learner dashboard as well as take the online tests which will instantly let you know your score and whether your ready to take the real test.

Welcome home, fellow citizen…

We wish you the very best of luck with the test and becoming a brand new British citizen. Britain is a vibrant, modern and diverse place to live with a wealth of cultures from the top at

John 'O Groats to the bottom at Lands End. Welcome home, sit yourself down and we'll put the kettle on!

Practice Test 1

1   What festival is celebrated on 31 October?

    A   Valentine's Day

    B   Bonfire Night

    C   Halloween

    D   Hogmanay

2   Is the statement below TRUE or FALSE?

The British constitution is contained in a single written document.

3   Which of the following statements is correct?

    A   *EastEnders* and *Coronation Street* are popular television programmes.

    B   *EastEnders* and *Coronation Street* are historical landmarks.

4   In 1999, what happened to hereditary peers in the House of Lords?

    A   Their numbers were greatly increased.

    B   Their salaries were stopped.

    C   Women were allowed to inherit their titles.

    D   They lost their automatic right to attend the House of Lords.

5   Is the statement below TRUE or FALSE?

Pantomimes are plays based on fairy stories.

6 Which TWO are political parties in the UK ?

  A Office Party

  B Modern Party

  C Conservative Party

  D Labour Party

7 How often does Prime Minister's Questions occur when Parliament is sitting?

  A Every day

  B Twice a week

  C Once a week

  D Once a month

8 Which of the following statements is correct?

  A The small claims procedure is an informal way of helping people to settle minor disputes.

  B The small claims procedure helps people to make small home insurance claims.

9 Which TWO are Protestant Christian groups in the UK?

  A Baptists

  B Methodists

  C Roman Catholics

  D Buddhists

10 What are TWO fundamental principles of British life?

  A Only driving your car on weekdays

  B Participation in community life

  C Growing your own fruit and vegetables

(**D**) Tolerance of those with different faiths and beliefs

11 Why is 1918 an important date in the history of women's rights?

    A   The first divorce laws were introduced.

    B   Women were given the right to vote.

    C   Equal pay laws were passed.

    D   Women were made legally responsible for their children.

12 Is the statement below TRUE or FALSE?

The National Citizen Service provides military training to young people.

13 For which TWO types of literature is William Shakespeare famous?

    A   Novels

    B   Plays

    C   Biographies

    D   Sonnets

14 Which of the following statements is correct?

    A   In 1588 the English defeated a Spanish invasion fleet of ships.

    B   In 1588 the English defeated a German invasion fleet of bomber planes.

15 What is the name of the UK currency?

    A   Dollar

    B   Euro

    C   Pound sterling

    D   Yen

16 Which TWO are members of Parliament (MPs) responsible for?

    A   Representing everyone in their constituency

B Scrutinising and commenting on what the government is doing

C Representing only those who voted for them

D Supporting the government on all decisions and laws

17 Which of the following statements is correct?

    A Most shops in the UK open seven days a week.

    B All shops in the UK close on Sundays.

18 Which TWO are English Civil War battles?

    A Waterloo

    B Marston Moor

    C Hastings

    D Naseby

19 Which of the following statements is correct?

    A Mary, Queen of Scots was unrelated to Queen Elizabeth I.

    B Mary, Queen of Scots was a cousin of Queen Elizabeth I.

20 Is the statement below TRUE or FALSE ?

    British scientists were the first to clone a mammal successfully. The animal was a rabbit.

21 Which TWO of the following do pressure and lobby groups do?

    A Organise violent protests

    B Influence government policy

    C Assist MPs in their constituency work

    D Represent the views of British businesses

22 Is the statement below TRUE or FALSE?

There is a dragon on the official flag of Wales.

23 What were the names of the TWO main groups in Parliament in the early 18th century?

    A   Whigs

    B   Labour

    C   Nationalists

    D   Tories

24 Which stories are associated with Geoffrey Chaucer?

    A   *The Westbury Tales*

    B   *The Ambridge Tales*

    C   *The London Tales*

    D   *The Canterbury Tales*

Practice Test 2

1 What important change to our voting rights took place in 1969?

    A   Women over 35 were given the vote.

    B   Prisoners were given the vote.

    C   The voting age was reduced to 18 for men and women.

    D   Compulsory voting was introduced.

2 Which TWO of the following are Christian religious festivals celebrated in the UK?

    A   Easter

    B   Halloween

    C   Christmas

D   New Year

3   Which of the following statements is correct?

    A   Self-employed people need to pay National Insurance Contributions themselves.

    B   Self-employed people can ask a friend to pay their National Insurance Contributions on their behalf.

4   How are local councils funded?

    A   Through money raised from local fundraising events

    B   Through donations from local people

    C   From central government and local taxes

    D   From local businesses

5   Which of the following statements is correct?

    A   Both Jane Austen and Charles Dickens are famous novelists.

    B   Both Jane Austen and Charles Dickens are famous painters.

6   What type of government was formed after the General Election of 2010?

    A   National

    B   All-party

    C   One-party

    D   Coalition

7   Which is an aim of the United Nations?

    A   To create a single free trade market

    B   To prevent war and promote international peace and security

    C   To examine decisions made by the European Union

    D   To promote dictatorship

8 Which of the following statements is correct?

    A The UK is governed by the parliament sitting in Westminster.

    B The UK is governed by parliaments sitting in Scotland, Wales and Northern Ireland.

9 Is the statement below TRUE or FALSE?

    The Brit Awards is an event where sports people are given awards.

10 What important event happened in England in 1066?

    A The Romans left England

    B The building of the Off a Dyke

    C The Norman invasion

    D The Battle of Bannockburn

11 Which of the following statements is correct?

    A The Divine Right of Kings' meant that the English king should rule France.

    B The Divine Right of Kings' meant that the king was appointed by God.

12 Which of the following is a fundamental principle of British life?

    A Extremism

    B Individual liberty

    C Intolerance

    D Inequality

13 Which TWO are famous UK landmarks?

    A Snowdonia

    B Grand Canyon

    C Loch Lomond

D   Notre Dame

14   Is the statement below TRUE or FALSE?

Members of the public are allowed to attend Youth Court hearings.

15   Which of the following statements is correct?

A   Elizabeth I handled Parliament very badly during her reign.

B   Elizabeth I had very good relations with Parliament.

16   What event is remembered on 5 November each year?

A   The end of the Second World War

B   The Queen's birthday

C   A plot to blow up the Houses of Parliament in 1605

D   The defeat of the Spanish Armada in 1588

17   Which TWO were associated with King Charles I and Parliament during the English Civil War?

A   Tories

B   Roundheads

C   Cavaliers

D   Luddites

18   Is the statement below TRUE or FALSE?   monarchy -

The Restoration' refers to the re-establishment of Catholicism as the official Church in the 17th century.

19   Which TWO are examples of civil law?

A   Disputes between landlords and tenants

B   Carrying a weapon

C   Discrimination in the workplace

D   Selling tobacco

20   Is the statement below TRUE or FALSE?

        The Scottish Parliament can pass legislation for Scotland on all matters.

21   Which of the following statements is correct?

        A   Gilbert and Sullivan were a comedy double act.

        B   Gilbert and Sullivan wrote many comic operas.

22   In 1999 which TWO new national bodies were established?

        A   House of Lords

        B   Welsh Assembly

        C   Scottish Parliament

        D   English Parliament

23   Is the statement below TRUE or FALSE?

        The Union Flag comprises four crosses, one for each part of the United Kingdom.

24   Is the statement below TRUE or FALSE?

        Some people rent land called 'an allotment', where they grow fruit and vegetables.

Practice Test 3

1   Is the statement below TRUE or FALSE?

        People are able to buy National Lottery tickets in the UK if they are aged 14 or over.

2   Why was Magna Carta important?

A   It gave all men the vote.

B   It limited the power of the monarch.

C   It established a new system of free education.

D   It gave women legal rights.

3   Which TWO types of case are held in County Courts?

A   Divorce

B   Murder

C   Minor criminal offences

D   Breaches of contract

4   Which of the following statements is correct?

A   The Industrial Revolution was the rapid development of industry in the 18th and 19th centuries.

B   The Industrial Revolution introduced changes in the banking system in the 1970s.

5   Who built the Tower of London?

A   Oliver Cromwell

B   Queen Elizabeth II

C   William the Conqueror

D   Winston Churchill

6   Which TWO chambers form the UK Parliament?

A House of Fraser

(B) House of Lords

(C) House of Commons

D House of Representatives

7 Which of the following statements is correct?

    A There is a yearly sailing race on the River Thames between Oxford and Cambridge Universities.

    (B) There is a yearly rowing race on the River Thames between Oxford and Cambridge Universities.

8 Which TWO are plays by William Shakespeare?

    (A) *A Midsummer Night's Dream*

    B *Pride and Prejudice*

    C *Romeo and Juliet*

    D *Oliver Twist*

9 Is the statement below TRUE or FALSE?

In 1805 at the Battle of Trafalgar, Admiral Nelson defeated the German fleet.

10   Which TWO issues can the devolved administrations pass laws on?

A   Health

B   Education

C   Foreign affairs

D   Immigration

11   Which of the following statements is correct?

A   UK laws ensure people are not treated unfairly in any area of work or life.

B   In the UK, employers can discriminate against different groups of people.

12   Is the statement below TRUE or FALSE?

Wales united with England during the reign of Henry VIII.

13   Which TWO are Christian groups?

A   Roman Catholics

B   Buddhists

C   Sikhs

D   Baptists

14   What TWO freedoms are offered by the UK to citizens and permanent residents?

A   Long lunch breaks on Friday

B   Freedom of speech

C   Free groceries for everyone

D   A right to a fair trial

15   When is a by-election for a parliamentary seat held?

     A   Half-way through a parliamentary term

     B   Every two years

     C   When a member of Parliament (MP) dies or resigns

     D   When the Prime Minister decides to call one

16   Which of the following statements is correct?

     A   Volunteering is a good way to earn additional money.

     B   Volunteering is a way of helping others without receiving payment.

17   Which is the most popular sport in the UK?

     A   Football

     B   Rugby

     C   Golf

     D   Tennis

18   Which of the following statements is correct?

A   Charles, king of Scotland, was restored as King Charles II of England in 1660.

B   Bonnie Prince Charlie became King Charles II of England in 1660.

19   Which TWO of the following do you have to pay tax on?

 A   Profits from self-employment

B   Income from property, savings and dividends

C   Shopping vouchers given to you by family or friends

D   Small amounts of money given to you as a gift

20   Which of the following statements is correct?

 A   The Proms is an eight-week summer season of orchestral music.

B   The Proms are a series of tennis matches held every June in London.

21   What were 'the Troubles' about?

A   Independence for Wales

B   Disagreement over Ireland becoming one country

C   Independence for Scotland

D   Setting up an English Parliament

22   Which TWO fought in wars against Napoleon?

A   Margaret Thatcher

B  Horatio Nelson

C Winston Churchill

D The Duke of Wellington

23 Is the statement below TRUE or FALSE?

Most people in the UK live in towns and cities.

24 What must you have done in order to vote in elections?

A Paid income tax in the previous year

B Put your name on the electoral register

C Registered your identity with the police

D Passed an electoral test

Practice Test 4

1 Which TWO are British overseas territories?

A Cyprus

B Falkland Islands

C St Helena

D Hawaii

2 Which of the following statements is correct?

A If your driving licence is from a country in the European Union you can drive in the UK for as long as your licence is valid.

B   If your driving licence is from a country in the European Union you have to apply for a UK licence in order to drive.

3   Which TWO of the following are famous British authors?

    A   Sir Steve Redgrave

    B   Gustav Holst

    C   Sir Arthur Conan Doyle

    D   J K Rawling

4   Which of the following statements is correct?

    A   In the 18th century two political groups emerged, the Whigs and the Tories.

    B   In the 18th century two political groups emerged, the Conservatives and the Liberals.

5   At what age can you vote in a General Election in the UK?

    A   16

    B   18

    C   21

    D   23

6   Which of the following statements is correct?

    A   Richard Arkwright developed new farming methods in the UK.

    B   Richard Arkwright developed efficient and profitable factories.

7   Which TWO services are funded by National Insurance Contributions?

    A   Local taxi services

    B   State retirement pension

    C   Supermarket home deliveries

    D   National Health Service (NHS)

8   In 1348 a third of the populations of England, Wales and Scotland died as a result of which plague?

  A   The Blue Death

  B   The White Death

  C   The Green Death

  (**D**)   The Black Death

9   Is the statement below TRUE or FALSE?

  In the UK, 1 April is a day when people play jokes on each other.

10   For which TWO reasons is Henry VIII remembered?

  A   Horse racing

  (**B**)   Married six times

  (**C**)   Broke away from the Church of Rome

  D   Had seven sons

11   Which TWO of the following are linked to football?

  A   The Ashes

  (**B**)   UEFA

  (**C**)   Premier League

  D   The Open

12   Which of the following statements is correct?

  (**A**)   Magistrates usually work unpaid and do not need legal qualifications.

  B   Magistrates must be specially trained legal experts who have been solicitors for three years.

13   Is the statement below TRUE or FALSE?

  When Queen Anne died, a German, George of Hanover, became the next king of England.

14   Which TWO festivals or traditions are held in November each year?

    A   Father's Day

    B   Valentine's Day

    C   Remembrance Day

    D   Bonfire Night

15   Is the statement below TRUE or FALSE?

Florence Nightingale is famous for her work on children's education in the 19th century.

16   Is the following statement TRUE or FALSE?

British values and principles are based on history and traditions.

17   Which of the following is a famous Stone Age site in the UK?

    A   Globe Theatre

    B   Nelson's Column

    C   Stonehenge

    D   Windsor Castle

18   St David is the patron saint of which country of the UK?

    A   England

    B   Scotland

    C   Wales

    D   Northern Ireland

19   Which TWO of the following are examples of criminal law?

    A   Racial crime

    B   Disputes about faulty goods

C Selling tobacco to anyone under the age of 18

D Discrimination in the workplace

20 Is the statement below TRUE or FALSE?

There are many variations in language in the different parts of the UK.

21 Where is the National Assembly for Wales based?

A London

B Newport

C Glasgow

D Cardiff

22 Textile and engineering firms recruited workers from which TWO countries after the Second World War?

A South Africa

B Canada

C India

D Pakistan

23 What is the name of a novel by Jane Austen?

A *Sense and Sensibility*

B *Far from the Madding Crowd*

C *Oliver Twist*

D *Our Man in Havana*

24 Is the statement below TRUE or FALSE?

The main political parties actively look for members.

Practice Test 5

1   Which of the following statements is correct?

    (A) Lancelot 'Capability' Brown and Gertrude Jekyll were famous garden designers.

    B   Lancelot 'Capability' Brown and Gertrude Jekyll were famous characters in a Sherlock Holmes story

2   How often are elections for the European Parliament held?

    A   Annually

    B   Every two years

    (C) Every five years

    D   Every 10 years

3   Which of the following is a country of the UK?

    A   Channel Islands

    (B) Scotland

    C   Isle of Man

    D   Republic of Ireland

4   Is the statement below TRUE or FALSE?

    Northern Ireland and Scotland have their own banknotes.

5   What is the minimum age you can drive a car or motor cycle in the UK?

    (A) 17

    B   21

    C   18

    D   25

6   How often are members of Parliament (MPs) elected?

   A   At least every three years

   B   Every six months

   C   Every year

   (D)   At least every five years

7   Which TWO political parties formed the coalition government in 2010?

   (A)   Conservatives

   B   Labour

   C   Communists

   (D)   Liberal Democrats

8   Which of the following statements is correct?

   (A)   The 'plantation' settlements in Ireland during the 17th century led to Protestant farmers replacing Catholic landowners.

   B   The 'plantation' settlements in Ireland during the 17th century led to Catholic farmers replacing Protestant landowners.

9   What are *Beowulf, The Tyger* and *She Walks in Beauty*?

   A   Plays

   B   Films

   (C)   Poems

   D   Novels

10   Which of the following statements is correct?

   (A)   The first person to use the title Prime Minister was Sir Robert Walpole.

   B   The first person to use the title Prime Minister was Sir Christopher Wren.

11   Is the statement below TRUE or FALSE?

Snowdonia is a national park in Northern Ireland.

12 Which language was spoken by people during the Iron Age?

    A   Latin

    B   Celtic

    C   English

    D   Anglo-Saxon

13 Which TWO records tell us about England during the time of William I?

    A   Domesday Book

    B   Diary of Samuel Pepys

    C   Magna Carta

    D   Bayeux Tapestry

14 Which event occurs each year on the third Sunday in June?

    A   Halloween

    B   Father's Day

    C   Boxing Day

    D   Remembrance Day

15 Is the statement below TRUE or FALSE?

A husband who forces his wife to have sex can be charged with rape.

16 Which form of religion developed as a result of the Reformation?

    A   Catholicism

    B   Protestantism

    C   Methodism

    D   Hinduism

17 Which of the following statements is correct?

    A   *The Mousetrap* is a play that has been running in London's West End since 1952.

    B   *The Mousetrap* is an environmental policy aiming to prevent mice from destroying crops.

18 Is the statement below TRUE or FALSE?

    In the UK a citizen may only follow an approved religion.

19 Which of the following is a traditional food associated with Scotland?

    A   Roast beef

    B   Ulster fry

    C   Fish and chips

    D   Haggis

20 Is the statement below TRUE or FALSE?

    Isaac Newton is a famous musician from the 18th century.

21 Which TWO of the following are major horse-racing events in the UK?

    A   The Open Championship

    B   Scottish Grand National

    C   Six Nations Championship

    D   Royal Ascot

22 Which of the following statements is correct?

    A   County Courts deal with criminal cases.

    B   County Courts deal with civil disputes.

23 Which TWO countries are members of the Commonwealth?

    A   USA

B Australia

C Canada

D Russia

24 Is the statement below TRUE or FALSE?

A public vote in 2002 decided that Winston Churchill was the Greatest Briton of all time.

Practice Test 6

1 Which TWO religions celebrate Diwali?

A Buddhists

B Hindus

C Christians

D Sikhs

2 Which of the following statements is correct?

A A free press means that what is written in newspapers is free from government control.

B A free press means newspapers are given out free of charge.

3 Is the statement below TRUE or FALSE? $10 - 17$

If a person is aged under 27, their case will be heard in a Youth Court.

4 Why was the Habeas Corpus Act of 1679 so important?

A It ensured no person could be held unlawfully.

B It allowed people to bury the dead where they wished.

C It ensured that those who died could only be buried by a relative.

D It ended capital punishment in England.

5 Which of the following is a Crown dependency?

    A   England

    B   Northern Ireland

    C   The Channel Islands

    D   Scotland

6 Which of the following statements is correct?

    A   The Speaker of the House of Commons remains a member of Parliament (MP) after election as Speaker.

    B   The Speaker of the House of Commons has to give up being an MP when elected as Speaker.

7 What awards event celebrates British theatre?

    A   The Laurence Olivier Awards

    B   The Turner Prize

    C   The Brit Awards

    D   The Man Booker Prize

8 Which TWO wars was England involved in during the Middle Ages?

    A   Crimean

    B   Crusades

    C   Hundred Years War

    D   Peninsular

9 Is the statement below TRUE or FALSE?

    Dundee and Aberdeen are cities in Northern Ireland.

10 How old do you need to be in order to stand for public office?

    A   16

B   18

C   20

D   21

11   Which of the following statements is correct?

     A   During Queen Elizabeth I's reign, English settlers began to colonise Australia.

     B   During Queen Elizabeth I's reign, English settlers began to colonise the eastern coast of North America

12   Which queen is remembered for her rebellion against the Romans?

     A   Elizabeth

     B   Boudicca

     C   Victoria

     D   Anne

13   Is the statement below   TRUE or FALSE?

     The jet engine and radar were developed in Britain in the 1830s.   1930

14   Which of the following statements is correct?

     A   Big Ben is a popular children's television character.

     B   Big Ben is the nickname of the great bell in the clock tower of the Houses of Parliament.

15   Which of the following statements is correct?

     A   Florence Nightingale is associated with policing.

     B   Florence Nightingale is associated with the development of nursing.

16   When walking your dog in a public place, what must you ensure?

     A   That your dog wears a special dog coat

     B   That your dog never strays more than 3 metres away from you

C   That your dog does not come into contact with other dogs

D   That your dog wears a collar showing the name and address of the owner

17   What did St Augustine and St Columba do during the Anglo-Saxon period?

     A   They invented new farming techniques.

     B   They were leaders of an uprising in Wales.

     C   They were early Christian missionaries.

     D   They were courageous warriors.

18   What is the role of a jury at a court trial?

     A   To decide whether evidence should be allowed to be heard

     B   To decide the sentence that the accused should be given

     C   To decide who the judge should be

     D   To decide whether the accused is 'guilty' or 'not guilty'

19   Which of the following statements is correct?

     A   A famous sailing event is held at Cowes on the Isle of Wight.

     B   A famous sailing event is held in the city of Belfast.

20   Is the statement below TRUE or FALSE?

     In the UK you are expected to respect the rights of others to have their own opinions.

21   Which TWO of the following are protected by law from discrimination?

     A   Disability

     B   Eye colour

     C   Choice of car

     D   Marital status

22 Which of the following statements is correct?

    A   The UK is a member of NATO.

    B   The UK has never been a member of NATO.

23 Which of the following statements is correct?

    A   The Industrial Revolution is the name given to the rapid development of industry in Britain in the 20th century.

    B   The Industrial Revolution is the name given to the rapid development of industry that began in the 18th century.

24 Which TWO events are religious festivals?

    A   Easter

    B   Christmas Day

    C   Boxing Day

    D   Bonfire Night

Practice Test 7

1 Who opens the new parliamentary session each year?

    A   The Archbishop of Canterbury

    B   The Prime Minister

    C   The Speaker of the House of Commons

    D   The monarch

2 Is the statement below TRUE or FALSE?

During the 18th century, radical new ideas about politics, philosophy and science were developed, called 'the Enlightenment'.

3 Is the statement below TRUE or FALSE?

The UK has a declining elderly population.

4 What TWO values are upheld by the Commonwealth association of countries?

A Democracy

B Communism

C Violence

D Rule of law

5 Which of the following statements is correct?

A Halloween is a modern American festival that has recently become popular in the UK.

B Halloween has its roots in an ancient pagan festival marking the beginning of winter.

6 Which TWO of the following were famous Victorians?

A Isambard Kingdom Brunel ~ *engineer*

B Margaret Thatcher

C Dylan Thomas

D Florence Nightingale

7 What countries does 'Great Britain' refer to?

A Just England

B England, Scotland and Wales

C England and Scotland

D England, Scotland and Northern Ireland   UK

8 Is the statement below TRUE or FALSE?

Forcing another person to marry is a criminal offence in the UK.

9 Which of the following statements is correct?

A The first professional UK football clubs were formed in the late 19th century.

B The first professional UK football clubs were formed in 1066.

10 What were TWO important aspects of the Reform Act of 1832?

A It decreased the power of the monarch.

B It increased the number of people who could vote.

C It abolished rotten boroughs

D It gave women the vote.

11 Is the statement below TRUE or FALSE?

Emmeline Pankhurst is famous for her leadership of the campaign to give women the vote in parliamentary elections in the UK.

12 Which TWO people are famous UK sports stars?

A Sir Chris Hoy

B Dame Kelly Holmes

C Lucien Freud

D Jane Austen

13 For approximately how many years did the Romans stay in this country?

A 50 years

B 100 years

C 400 years

D 600 years

14 Which of the following statements is correct?

A Members of Parliament (MPs) are elected through a system called 'first past the post'.

B MPs are elected through a system called 'the winner takes it all'.

15   Is the statement below TRUE or FALSE

The 40 days before Easter are known as Lent.

16   Is the statement below TRUE or FALSE?

The 'Swinging Sixties' is associated with the 1860s.

17   Which TWO of the following are major outdoor music festivals?

  A   Royal Ascot

  B   Isle of Wight Festival

  C   Hogmanay

  D   Glastonbury

18   Where did the Vikings come from?

  A   Germany and Austria

  B   Belgium and Holland

  C   Denmark and Norway

  D   France and Luxembourg

19   Which of the following statements is correct?

  A   Sake Dean Mahomet is famous for introducing tea-drinking and bungalows to Britain from India.

  B   Sake Dean Mahomet introduced curry houses and shampooing to Britain from India.

20   Which TWO principles are included in the European Convention on Human Rights?

  A   Prohibition of slavery and forced labour

  B   Freedom of thought, conscience and religion

  C   The right to use violence if you think it is necessary

  D   Freedom to leave work early every Friday

39

21 St Andrew is the patron saint of which country?

   A   England

   B   Scotland

   C   Wales

   D   Northern Ireland

22 Is the following statement TRUE or FALSE?

   There is a no place in British society for extremism or intolerance.

23 Which of the following statements is correct?

   A   The public can attend debates in the House of Commons.

   B   No member of the public is allowed to attend debates in the House of Commons.

24 By joining a political party, what TWO activities might you be involved in?

   A   Violent clashes with other political parties

   B   Joining your MP for sessions in the House of Commons

   C   Handing out leaflets in the street

   D   Knocking on people's doors and asking for support

Practice Test 8

1 What do Sir william Golding, Seamus Heaney and Harold Pinter have in common?

   A   They are all famous British athletes.

   B   They have all been Prime Minister.

   C   They were part of the first British expedition to the North Pole.

   D   They have all been awarded the Nobel Prize for literature.

2 Who elects Police and Crime Commissioners (PCCs)?

A The police

B The Home Office

(C) The public

D Members of Parliament

3 Which of the following statements is correct?

(A) The Reform Act of 1832 increased the number of electors.

B The Reform Act of 1832 increased the power of the House of Lords.

4 What celebration takes place each year on 14 February?

(A) Valentine's Day

B Bonfire Night

C Halloween

D Hogmanay

5 Which TWO of the following issues can the Northern Ireland Assembly make decisions on?

A Defence

B Agriculture

C Foreign affairs

D Social services

6 Is the statement below TRUE or FALSE? Spanish

In 1588 the English fleet defeated a large French fleet of ships that intended to land an army in England.

7 Who was given the title of Lord Protector in the 17th century?

A King Charles II

B Samuel Pepys

C Oliver Cromwell

D Isaac Newton

8   Is the statement below TRUE or FALSE?

We shall fight them on the beaches' is a famous quote from a speech by Queen Elizabeth I about the Spanish Armada.

9   What system of government does the UK have?

A Communist government

B Dictatorship

C Parliamentary democracy

D Federal government

10   Which of the following statements is correct?

A In 1776 some American colonies declared their independence from Britain.

B American colonists were eventually defeated by the British.

11   When a member of Parliament (MP) dies or resigns, what is the election called that is held to replace them?

A Re-selection

B Selection

C Hustings

D By-election

12   Which TWO of the following were British inventions?

A Television

B Jet engine

C Personal computer

D   Diesel engine

13   Which of the following UK landmarks is in Northern Ireland?

    A   Big Ben

    B   Snowdonia

    C   The Giant's Causeway

    D   The Eden Project

14   Who has to pay National Insurance Contributions?

    A   Everybody in the UK who is in paid work

    B   People who work full-time

    C   All those aged 50 and below

    D   Single people with no dependents

15   Which of the following statements is correct?

    A   Civil servants are politically neutral.

    B   Civil servants have to be politically aligned to the elected government.

16   Is the statement below TRUE or FALSE?

Mo Farah and Jessica Ennis are well-known athletes who won gold medals at the 2012 London Olympics.

17   How old must you be to ride a moped in the UK?

    A   18

    B   25

    C   16

    D   21

18   Is the statement below TRUE or FALSE?

Getting to know your neighbours can help you to become part of the community.

19 Which of the following statements is correct?

    A Sir Steve Redgrave is a famous rower who won gold medals in five consecutive Olympic Games.

    B Sir Steve Redgrave is a famous film actor who has won several BAFTAs.

20 When was the last successful invasion of England?

    A 1066

    B 1415

    C 1642

    D 1940

21 Which TWO patron saints' days occur in March?

    A St David

    B St Patrick

    C St George

    D St Andrew

22 Is the statement below TRUE or FALSE?

    John Constable (1776-1837) founded the modern police force in England.

23 Which TWO are 20th-century British discoveries or inventions?

    A Hovercraft

    B Radium

    C Penicillin

    D Printing press

24 Which of the following statements is correct?

A The UK offers its citizens and permanent residents freedom of speech.

B The UK does not allow citizens or permanent residents to voice opinions publicly.

Practice Test 9

1 Is the statement below TRUE or FALSE?

Participating in your community is a fundamental principle of British life.

2 On which date is St Patrick's Day celebrated?

A 1 March

B 17 March

C 23 April

D 30 November

3 Which of the following statements is correct?

A After the age of 70, drivers must renew their licence every three years.

B After the age of 70, drivers must renew their licence every five years.

4 Which TWO foods are associated with England?

A Haggis

B Ulster fry

C Roast beef

D Fish and chips

5 Which of the following statements is correct?

A During the First World War Winston Churchill was the British Prime Minister.

B During the Second World War Winston Churchill was the British Prime Minister.

6 If your car is more than three years old, how often will it need a Ministry of Transport (MOT) test?

    A Every three years

    B Every six months

    C Every 10 years

    D Every year

7 Who were the 'suffragettes'?

    A Women who left the UK to live in India

    B Women who campaigned for women's votes

    C Women who chose to be single

    D Women who stayed at home to raise a family

8 Which of the following statements is correct?

    A Andy Murray is the first British man to sail around the world.

    B Andy Murray is the first British man to win a singles tennis title in a Grand Slam tournament since 1936.

9 Is the statement below TRUE or FALSE?

All young people are sent a National Insurance number just before their 16th birthday.

10 Which TWO changes were introduced by the Education Act of 1944?

    A New public examinations

    B Primary education for all

    C Free secondary education for all

    D A clear division between primary and secondary education

11 Which of the following is a British overseas territory?

A Northern Ireland

B The Falkland Islands

C France

D USA

12 Which TWO are 20th-century British discoveries or inventions?

A Cloning a mammal

B Cash machines (ATMs)

C Mobile phones

D Walkmans

13 Which of the following statements is correct?

A Members of the House of Lords are not elected by the people.

B Members of the House of Lords are voted in by members of the House of Commons.

14 Which Scottish king defeated the English at the Battle of Bannockburn in 1314?

A William Wallace

B Robert the Bruce

C Malcolm

D Andrew

15 Is the statement below TRUE or FALSE?

Thomas Hardy is a famous author who wrote Far from the Madding Crowd.

16 Which of the following statements is correct?

A George and Robert Stephenson were famous pioneers of railway engines.

B George and Robert Stephenson were famous pioneers of agricultural changes.

17 Is the statement below TRUE or FALSE?

During the Victorian period the British Empire became the largest empire the world has ever seen.

18 Which TWO of the following are UK landmarks?

A The Eisteddfod

B National Trust

C Edinburgh Castle

D The London Eye

19 Is the statement below TRUE or FALSE?

Wales, Scotland and Northern Ireland each have devolved administrations which give them total control over all policies and laws.

20 Which TWO things can you do to look after the environment?

A Drive your car as much as possible

B Recycle your waste

C Never turn the lights off in your house

D Walk and use public transport to get around

21 Which of the following statements is correct?

A National parks are areas of protected countryside that everyone can visit.

B National parks are national sports grounds for people to hold sporting events.

22 Is the statement below TRUE or FALSE?

Before 1215 there were no laws to limit the power of the king of England.

23 What is the capital city of wales?

A Swansea

B Cardiff

C Edinburgh

D Belfast

22 / 24

24 What is a jury made up of?

A People working in high-powered jobs

B People randomly chosen from the electoral register

C People who are members of political parties

D People who have submitted an application form and been accepted

Practice Test 10

1 What was Isambard Kingdom Brunei famous for designing and building?

A Motor cars

B Aeroplanes

C Bridges

D Skyscrapers

2 Which TWO of the following would you contact for legal advice?

A A solicitor

B A local councillor

C The Citizens Advice Bureau

D Your local member of Parliament (MP)

3 Which of the following statements is correct?

A The official home of the Prime Minister is 10 Downing Street.

B   The official home of the Prime Minister is Buckingham Palace.

4   Is the statement below TRUE or FALSE?

Charles Dickens is famous for writing musicals.

5   How many people serve on a jury in Scotland?

    A   8

    B   11

    C   (15)

    D   20

15 - Scotland
12 - in England

6   At which festival are mince pies traditionally eaten?

    A   Easter

    B   Diwali

    C   Christmas

    D   Vaisakhi

7   Which TWO of the following groups of adults are eligible to vote in all UK elections?

    A   UK-born and naturalised adult citizens

    B   Only those born in the UK

    C   Citizens of the Commonwealth who are resident in the UK

    D   Citizens of the USA

8   What task is associated with the National Trust?

    A   Conserving native bird species

    B   Preserving old aircraft

    C   Preserving important buildings and places

    D   Conserving deep water fish

9   Who appoints life peers in the House of Lords?

    A   The monarch

    B   The Prime Minister

    C   The Speaker of the House of Commons

    D   The Chief Whip

10   Which TWO of the following were major welfare changes introduced from 1945 to 1950?

    A   National Health Service (NHS)

    B   State retirement pension

    C   Employment exchanges

    D   A social security system for all

11   Which of the following statements is correct?

    A   Rugby was introduced to ancient Britain by Viking invaders.

    B   Rugby originated in England in the early 19th century.

12   To which TWO international bodies does the UK belong?

    A   The North Atlantic Treaty Organization (NATO)

    B   The Commonwealth

    C   The North American Free Trade Agreement (NAFTA)

    D   The Arab League

13   Which of the following statements is correct?

    A   The 'Swinging Sixties' was a period of religious change.

    B   The 'Swinging Sixties' was a period of social change.

14   What is the highest-value note issued as British currency?

    A   £20

B   £70

C   £50

D   £100

15 Is the statement below TRUE or FALSE?

> You can support your local community by becoming a school governor or
> school board member.

16 Which of the following statements is correct?

    A   The Reform Act of 1832 decreased the number of voters.

    B   The Reform Act of 1832 increased the number of voters.

17 Which TWO are famous gardens in the UK?

    A   London Eye

    B   Sissinghurst

    C   Bodnant Garden

    D   Snowdonia

18 Which of the following statements is correct?

    A   The Queen is ceremonial head of the Commonwealth.

    B   The Queen is ceremonial head of the North Atlantic Treaty Organization (NATO).

19 Why is Henry VIII an important English monarch?

    A   He broke from the Church of Rome.

    B   He established the RAF.

    C   He invaded Sweden.

    D   He re-established the Catholic Church in England.

20 Is the statement below TRUE or FALSE??

William Blake, Lord Byron and Robert Browning were all famous golfers.

21 Is the statement below TRUE or FALSE?

In 1921 a treaty gave independence to the south of Ireland.

22 Which TWO were introduced before the First World War (1914)?

A National Health Service (NHS)

B Child Benefit payments

C State retirement pension

D Free school meals

23 Which of the following statements is correct?

A Cricket matches can last up to five days.

B Cricket matches can last up to two weeks.

24 Is the statement below TRUE or FALSE?

Britain has never been at war with France.

Practice Test 11

1 Which TWO are associated with Sir Francis Drake?

A The Spanish Armada

B Early flight

C *The Titanic*

D Sailing around the world

2 Which jubilee did Queen Elizabeth II celebrate in 2012?

A Platinum Jubilee

B   Diamond Jubilee

C   Silver Jubilee

D   Golden Jubilee

3   Which of the following statements is correct?

      A   In 1998 the Good Friday Agreement devolved powers to Wales.

      B   In 1998 the Good Friday Agreement led to the establishment of the Northern Ireland Assembly.

4   Which is the UK's most popular sport?

      A   Cricket

      B   Golf

      C   Rugby

      D   Football

5   Which of the following statements is correct?

      A   On becoming a UK citizen or permanent resident, you can choose which laws and responsibilities you want to accept.

      B   On becoming a UK citizen or permanent resident, you will be agreeing to respect the laws, values and traditions of the UK.

6   Is the statement below TRUE or FALSE?

      The daffodil is the national flower of Wales.

7   Which area of government policy is the responsibility of the Chancellor of the Exchequer?

      A   Education

      B   Health

      C   Economy

      D   Legal affairs

8   Dunkirk is associated with which TWO events?

       A   Landings on D-Day

       B   The fall of Singapore

       C   The rescue of 300,000 men

       D   Small boats coming to the rescue

9   Which is the capital city of the UK?

       A   Westminster

       B   Birmingham

       C   Windsor

       D   London

10   Which of the following statements is correct?

       A   In the UK organ donation is a legal requirement

       B   In the UK organ donation is voluntary.

11   What are the titles of TWO novels by Charles Dickens?

       A   *Harry Potter*

       B   *Pride and Prejudice*

       C   *Great Expectations*

       D   *Oliver Twist*

12   which of the following statements is correct?

       A   The Battle of Britain in 1940 was fought at sea.

       B   The Battle of Britain in 1940 was fought in the skies.

13   What was the name given to supporters of King Charles I during the Civil War?

       A   Luddites

B Roundheads

C Cavaliers

D Levellers

14 which of the following statements is correct?

    A The Roman army left England after 150 years to defend other parts of their Empire.

    B The Roman army left England after 400 years to defend other parts of their Empire.

15 How can you reduce your carbon footprint?

    A Shop locally for products

    B Buy duty-free products when you're abroad

    C Do all your shopping online

    D Drive to the supermarket

16 Is the statement below TRUE or FALSE?

A traditional food in Wales is Ulster fry.

17 Of which product did the UK produce over half the world's supply in the 19th century?

    A Cotton cloth

    B Beer

    C Cigarettes

    D Rubber

18 Is the statement below TRUE or FALSE?

Members of the armed forces cannot stand for public office.

19 What are TWO benefits of volunteering?

    A Earning additional money

B   Meeting new people

C   You are given a courtesy car as transport

D   Making your community a better place

20   Is the statement below TRUE or FALSE?

The Civil War between Charles I and Parliament in the mid-17th century led to Oliver Cromwell becoming king of England.

21   Which TWO of the following are famous British artists?

A   Andy Murray

B   David Hockney

C   Sir Edward Elgar

D   Henry Moore

22   Is the statement below TRUE or FALSE?

You can serve on a jury up to the age of 80.

23   Which of the following statements is correct?

A   The official Church of state of the UK is the Church of England.

B   There is no official Church in the UK.

24   Which TWO of the following are part of the UK government?

A   The cabinet

B   The civil service

C   The National Trust

D   FIFA

Practice Test 12

1   Is the statement below TRUE or FALSE?

In the 1830s and 1840s a group called the Chartists campaigned for reform to the voting system.

2   During the 'Great Depression' of the 1930s, which TWO major new industries developed?

      A   Shipbuilding

      B   Coal mining

      C   Automobile

      D   Aviation

3   Once you are aged 17 or older, which TWO vehicles can you learn to drive?

      A   Motor cycle

      B   Car

      C   Fire engine

      D   Heavy goods vehicle

4   The Bill of Rights of 1689 limited whose powers?

      A   The king

      B   Parliament

      C   Judges

      D   The Church

5   Which of the following statements is correct?

      A   The capital cities of the nations of the UK are London, Swansea, Glasgow and Dublin.

      B   The capital cities of the nations of the UK are London, Cardiff, Edinburgh and Belfast

6   Is the statement below TRUE or FALSE?

In 1707 the kingdoms of England and Scotland were united.

7   To apply for UK citizenship or permanent residency, which TWO things do you need?

   A   A UK bank account

   B   An ability to speak and read English

   C   A good understanding of life in the UK

   D   A driving licence

8   Which of the following statements is correct?

   A   The Anglo-Saxon kingdoms in England were united under King Alfred the Great.

   B   The Anglo-Saxon kingdoms were united under King Kenneth MacAlpin.

9   Is the statement below TRUE or FALSE?

   The court systems in England, Wales, Scotland and Northern Ireland are identical.

10   Is the statement below TRUE or FALSE?

   The British Broadcasting Corporation (BBC) is financed by selling advertising space during television programmes.

11   What happens when members of Parliament (MPs) hold surgeries?

   A   They meet local councillors to discuss local issues.

   B   Members of the public can meet their MP to discuss issues.

   C   They discuss local health issues with doctors.

   D   They invite members of the press along to talk over national issues.

12   Which of the following statements is correct?

   A   Hadrian's Wall was built on the orders of the Roman Emperor Hadrian.

   B   Hadrian's Wall was built by the Picts (ancestors of the Scottish people) to keep out the Romans.

13   Which TWO famous London buildings are built in the 19th-century 'gothic' style?

A St Paul's Cathedral

B The Houses of Parliament

C St Pancras Station

D Buckingham Palace

14 Is the statement below TRUE or FALSE?

King Henry VIII created the Church of England when the Pope refused to grant him a divorce.

15 Which TWO developments are associated with the 'Swinging Sixties'?

A Children's rights law reform

B Abortion law reform

C Divorce law reform

D Decimal currency

16 What type of church is the Church of Scotland?

A Quaker

B Roman Catholic

C Presbyterian

D Methodist

17 Is the statement below TRUE or FALSE?

St Helena is a Crown dependency.

18 Which TWO of the following are traditional British foods?

A Strudel

B Sushi

C Welsh cakes

D   Haggis

19   Which of the following statements is correct?

       A   An example of a criminal offence is carrying a weapon.

       B   An example of a criminal offence is being in debt.

20   Bobby Moore is famous for his achievements in which sport?

       A   Football

       B   Rugby union

       C   Horse racing

       D   Motor racing

21   Is the statement below TRUE or FALSE?

If you are an EU citizen living in the UK you can vote in all British public elections.

22   The term 'suffragettes' is associated with which group of people?

       A   Men

       B   Women

       C   Children

       D   Migrants

23   which of the following statements is correct?

       A   Wales and Northern Ireland each have their own Church of state.

       B   There is no established Church in Wales or Northern Ireland.

24   which court would you use to get money back that was owed to you?

       A   County Court

       B   Magistrates' Court

C   Youth Court

D   Coroner's Court

Practice Test 13

1   Which TWO are famous British fashion designers?

    A   Mary Quant

    B   Capability Brown

    C   Edwin Lutyens

    D   Vivienne Westwood

2   Henry VII established the House of Tudor. What colour rose became the Tudor emblem?

    A   White

    B   Red and white

    C   Red

    D   Pink

3   Which of the following statements is correct?

    A   By the middle of the 17th century the last Welsh rebellions had been defeated.

    B   By the middle of the 15th century the last Welsh rebellions had been defeated.

4   What TWO actions can a judge take if a public body is not respecting someone's legal rights?

    A   Place its members in prison

    B   Order them to change their practices

    C   Order them to pay compensation

D Close down the public body

5 In everyday language people may say, 'rain stopped play'. With which sport is this phrase associated?

A Football

B Cricket

C Rugby league

D Horse racing

6 Which of the following statements is correct?

A The Battle of Agincourt is commemorated in the Bayeux Tapestry.

B The Battle of Hastings is commemorated in the Bayeux Tapestry.

7 Is the statement below TRUE or FALSE?

Shakespeare was a great English playwright.

8 Which TWO courts deal with minor criminal cases in the UK?

A Justice of the Peace Court

B Centre Court

C Crown Court

D Magistrates' Court

9 What is a fundamental principle of British life?

A The rule of law

B The rule of the upper classes

C The rule of the monarch

D The rule of your local member of Parliament (MP)

10 Is the statement below TRUE or FALSE?

In 1833 a law abolished slavery throughout the British Empire.

11 Which TWO of the following were important 20th-century inventors?

    A Alan Turing

    B Tim Berners-Lee

    C George Stephenson

    D Isambard Kingdom Brunel

12 Which sport can be traced back to 15th-century Scotland?

    A Surfing

    B Formula 1

    C Golf

    D Motorbike racing

13 What must police officers do?

    A Be rude and abusive

    B Obey the law

    C Make a false statement

    D Be politically neutral

14 What is the title of the UK National Anthem?

    A Long Live the Queen

    B God Save the Queen

    C Long Live the Monarch

    D Almighty is the Queen

15 Is the statement below TRUE or FALSE?

People over 75 years of age do not have to pay for a television licence.

16 The Union Flag consists of three crosses. One is St George's. Who do the other TWO crosses represent?

    A   St David

    B   St Patrick

    C   St Andrew

    D   St Piran

17 Who do some local councils appoint as a ceremonial leader?

    A   A local business leader

    B   A member of the Royal Family

    C   A local celebrity

    D   A mayor

18 Which of the following statements is correct?

    A   Baptists. Methodists and Quakers are all linked to the Roman Catholic Church.

    B   Baptists, Methodists, and Quakers are Protestant Christian groups.

19 Is the statement below TRUE or FALSE?

The Channel Islands are a part of the UK.

20 D-Day refers to what event in British history?

    A   Battle of Trafalgar

    B   British invasion of Europe in 1944

    C   Dropping of the atom bomb on Japan

    D   End of the war in Europe in 1945

21 Which of the following statements is correct?

    A   The capital city of Northern Ireland is Swansea.

B The capital city of Northern Ireland is Belfast.

22 Which TWO plants are associated with the UK?

    A Shamrock

    B Rose

    C Cactus

    D Olive tree

23 Which of the following statements is correct?

    A There are a few members of Parliament who do not represent any of the main political parties.

    B All members of Parliament have to belong to a political party

24 Is the statement below TRUE or FALSE?

The Home Secretary is the government minister responsible for managing relationships with foreign countries.

Practice Test 14

1 Which part of the UK is associated with Robert Burns (1759-96)?

    A England

    B Scotland

    C Wales

    D Northern Ireland

2 Which TWO developments were features of the Industrial Revolution?

    A Machinery

    B Medical advances

    C Changes in the law

D   Steam power

3   Which of the following statements is correct?

    A   Several British writers have won the Nobel Prize in Literature.

    B   No British writer has won the Nobel Prize in Literature.

4   What is one of the roles of school governors and school boards?

    A   Setting the strategic direction of the school

    B   Marking students' homework

    C   Giving teachers ideas for lesson plans

    D   Serving food and drink in the canteen

5   After the abolition of slavery, more than 2 million migrants came from which TWO countries to replace the freed slaves?

    A   Russia

    B   India

    C   China

    D   Australia

6   Is the statement below TRUE or FALSE?

    In the UK betting and gambling are illegal.

7   In which part of the British Empire did the Boer War of 1899-1902 take place?

    A   India

    B   Canada

    C   Australia

    D   South Africa

8   Which of the following statements is correct?

A By 1400 the preferred language of the English court was French.

B By 1400 the preferred language of the English court was English.

9 What are the names of TWO famous British film actors?

    A Tilda Swinton

    B Jayne Torvill

    C Colin Firth

    D Robert Louis Stevenson

10 Which of the following statements is correct?

    A The capital city of Scotland is Edinburgh.

    B The capital city of Scotland is Glasgow.

11 What sort of cases do Crown Courts and Sheriff Courts deal with?

    A Small claims procedures

    B Youth cases

    C Minor criminal cases

    D Serious offences

12 In which modern-day country was the composer George Frederick Handel born?

    A Iceland

    B Russia

    C Japan

    D Germany

13 What is the minimum age for jury service?

    A 22

    B 18

C   16

D   30

14   Which of the following statements is correct?

    A   Proceedings in Parliament cannot be reported in the press.

    B   Proceedings in Parliament are broadcast on television.

15   Is the statement below TRUE or FALSE?

The Lake District is England's largest national park.

16   Which of the following statements is correct?

    A   The Black Death was a plague that only had an impact in Ireland, where many people died.

    B   The Black Death brought about major changes in English society due to the number of people who died.

17   Is the statement below TRUE or FALSE?

Henry VIII is famous for marrying six times and breaking away from the Church of Rome.

18   Since 1927 the BBC has organised which series of famous concerts?

    A   The Eisteddfod

    B   Aldeburgh Festival

    C   The Proms

    D   Glastonbury

19   Which TWO are famous horse-racing events?

    A   The Grand National

    B   The Cup Final

    C   Royal Ascot

    D   The Six Nations

20 Which of the following statements is correct?

    A   Decisions on government policies are made by the monarch.

    B   Decisions on government policies are made by the Prime Minister and cabinet.

21 Is the statement below TRUE or FALSE?

The Isle of Man is a Crown dependency

22 In which battle during the First World War did the British suffer 60, 000 casualties on the first day?

    A   Agincourt

    B   El Alamein

    C   The Somme

    D   Waterloo

23 Is the statement below TRUE or FALSE?

Pressure and lobby groups try to influence British government policy

24 who are TWO famous British film directors?

    A   Sir Alfred Hitchcock

    B   Evelyn Waugh

    C   Ridley Scott

    D   Thomas Gainsborough

Practice Test 15

1 Which group of refugees settled in England before 1720?

    A   Welsh

    B   Germans

C   Bretons

D   Huguenots

2   Which TWO are 20th-century British discoveries or inventions?

     A   Television

     B   World wide Web

     C   Mobile phone

     D   Diesel engine

3   During which part of the year are pantomime productions staged in theatres?

     A   Easter

     B   Summer

     C   Christmas

     D   Valentine's Day

4   Which of the following statements is correct?

     A   The civil service largely consists of political appointees.

     B   The civil service is politically neutral.

5   Is the statement below TRUE or FALSE?

     An example of a civil law case is when you have purchased a faulty item and made a legal complaint.

6   Which TWO of the following are famous Paralympians?

     A   Jessica Ennis

     B   Ellie Simmonds

     C   Baroness Tanni Grey-Thompson

     D   Dame Ellen MacArthur

7 How is the Speaker of the House of Commons chosen?

    A By the monarch

    B Through a public election

    C In a secret ballot

    D By the Prime Minister

8 Is the statement below TRUE or FALSE?

Margaret Thatcher was the longest-serving UK Prime Minister of the 20th century.

9 Which of the following statements is correct?

    A Police and Crime Commissioners (PCCs) are appointed through a public election.

    B Police and Crime Commissioners (PCCs) are appointed by the local council.

10 Which of the following statements is correct?

    A The BBC is funded through advertisements and subscriptions.

    B The BBC is the only wholly state-funded media organisation

11 Which TWO members of a family have a special day dedicated to them?

    A Uncles

    B Fathers

    C Mothers

    D Aunts

12 Which of the following statements is correct?

    A It is free to visit the Houses of Parliament to watch debates.

    B It costs £15 per person to visit the Houses of Parliament to watch debates.

13 Which TWO responsibilities should you respect as a resident of the UK?

A   Respect and obey the law

B   Treat others with fairness

C   Vote for the government in power

D   Take in and look after stray animals

14   Which country did Germany invade in 1939 that led to the UK declaring war on Germany?

     A   Austria

     B   Finland

     C   Poland

     D   France

15   Which of the following statements is correct?

     A   The Wars of the Roses were between the Houses of Lancaster and York.

     B   The Wars of the Roses were between the Houses of windsor and Tudor.

16   Is the statement below TRUE or FALSE?

     Most people live in the countryside in the UK.

17   Dylan Thomas was a famous writer and poet from which country?

     A   England

     B   Scotland

     C   Wales

     D   Northern Ireland

18   Which of the following statements is correct?

     A   You have to be aged 18 or over to buy a National Lottery ticket.

     B   You have to be aged 16 or over to buy a National Lottery ticket.

19   Which of the following do you need in order to gain a full car licence?

    A   Pass a driving test which tests both knowledge and practical skills

    B   Own a car

    C   Achieve five GCSE passes

    D   Be in employment

20   Which of the following statements is correct?

    A   James VI of Scotland was related to Queen Elizabeth I of England.

    B   James VI of Scotland was not related to Queen Elizabeth I of England.

21   Is the statement below TRUE or FALSE?

The Crown Jewels are kept at the Tower of London.

22   Which TWO points about slavery are correct?

    A   William Wilberforce was a leading abolitionist.

    B   Slavery survived in the British Empire until the early 20th century.

    C   Quakers set up the first anti-slavery groups.

    D   The Royal Navy refused to stop ships carrying slaves.

23   Which of the following statements is correct?

    A   The UK is made up of the following countries : England, Scotland, Wales and Ireland.

    B   The UK is made up of the following countries: England, Scotland, Wales and Northern Ireland.

24   Which of the following areas does civil law cover?

    A   Debt

    B   Violent crime

    C   Burglary

D   Drunk and disorderly behaviour

Practice Test 16

1   Is the statement below TRUE or FALSE?

During the Great Depression of the 7930s the UK had high levels of employment.

2   Which of the following statements is correct?

    A   The Chancellor of the Exchequer is responsible for crime, policing and immigration.

    B   The Chancellor of the Exchequer is responsible for the economy.

3   Which colonies of the British Empire decided to declare their independence in 1776?

    A   Australian

    B   Canadian

    C   American

    D   South African

4   What is the minimum legal age you can buy alcohol in the UK?

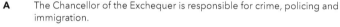

    A   20

    B   16

    C   18

    D   19

5   Is the statement below TRUE or FALSE?

The Wimbledon Championships are associated with motor sports.

6   Which TWO were great thinkers of the Enlightenment?

A   Robert Burns

B   Robert Louis Stevenson

C   Adam Smith

D   David Hume

7   With which sport do you associate Lewis Hamilton, Jensen Button and Damon Hill?

    A   Football

    B   Athletics

    C   Skiing

    D   Formula 1

8   What happens when a member of Parliament (MP) dies or resigns?

    A   The post remains vacant until the next General Election.

    B   Their party chooses someone to fill the post until the next General Election.

    C   A by-election is held to replace the MP.

    D   A neighbouring MP looks after the constituency.

9   Which of the following statements is correct?

    A   Plymouth, Norwich and Leeds are cities in England.

    B   Newport, Swansea and Cardiff are cities in Scotland.

10   Is the statement below TRUE or FALSE?

    The House of Lords always acts as the government wishes.

11   Which TWO are famous British authors?

    A   Thomas Hardy

    B   Graham Greene

C   Mary Quant

D   Henry Moore

12   Who invaded England in 1066?

     A   Richard the Lionheart

     B   Canute

     C   William of Normandy

     D   Harold of Wessex

13   Which TWO genres is william Shakespeare famous for writing?

     A   Plays

     B   TV dramas

     C   Poems

     D   Radio scripts

14   Which of the following statements is correct?

     A   The National Trust is a charity that works to preserve important buildings in the UK.

     B   The National Trust is a government-run organisation that provides funding for charities.

15   What is a responsibility that you will have as a citizen or permanent resident of the UK?

     A   To keep your dog on a lead at all times

     B   To avoid shopping on a Sunday

     C   To look after yourself and your family

     D   To grow your own vegetables

16   Is the statement below TRUE or FALSE?

A General Election occurs every eight years.

17   What happened to Margaret Thatcher in 1979 to make her famous in UK history?

    A   She took part in the Olympics.

    B   She became a High Court judge.

    C   She became the first woman Prime Minister.

    D   She was made a general in the British army.

18   Which TWO are influential British bands?

    A   The National Trust

    B   The Rolling Stones

    C   The Beatles

    D   The Royal Family

19   Which of the following statements is correct?

    A   In Northern Ireland a member of your family must complete a voting registration form on your behalf.

    B   In Northern Ireland all those entitled to vote must complete their own registration form.

20   What is a bank holiday?

    A   A public holiday when banks and other businesses close for the day

    B   A holiday just for people working in banks

    C   A week off for everyone in the UK

    D   An extra holiday entitlement for working longer hours than usual

21   Which of the following statements is correct?

    A   The Highland Clearances occurred in Scotland.

    B   The Highland Clearances occurred in Ireland.

22   What is a traditional pub game in the UK?

A   Scrabble

B   Pool

C   Rounders

D   Poker

23   Which of the following statements is correct?

      A   Henry VIII established the Church of England in order to start a war with the French.

      B   Henry VIII established the Church of England because the Pope refused to grant him a divorce.

24   Is the statement below TRUE or FALSE?

      Boys in the UK leave school with better qualifications than girls.

Practice Test 17

1   Hadrian's Wall was built to keep out whom?

      A   The Irish

      B   The Welsh

      C   The Picts

      D   The Vikings

2   Which of the following statements is correct?

      A   Shakespeare wrote 'To be or not to be'.

      B   Shakespeare wrote 'We will fight them on the beaches'.

3   The Enlightenment led to major developments in which TWO areas?

      A   Science

      B   Politics

C   History

D   Theatre

4   Which of the following statements is correct?

    A   All Acts of Parliament are made in the monarch's name.

    B   All Acts of Parliament are made in the Prime Minister's name.

5   Why is Sir Edwin Lutyens famous?

    A   He won a gold medal at the London 2012 Olympic Games.

    B   He was the first UK Prime Minister.

    C   He invented the World wide Web.

    D   He was a 20th-century architect.

6   Is the statement below TRUE or FALSE?

    The First World War ended at 11. 00 am on 11 November 1918.

7   Which TWO groups contested the Wars of the Roses in the 15th century?

    A   Irish

    B   House of York

    C   Scottish

    D   House of Lancaster

8   Which parts of the United Kingdom have devolved governments?

    A   England and Wales

    B   Wales, England and Northern Ireland

    C   Only Northern Ireland

    D   Wales, Scotland and Northern Ireland

9   Is the statement below TRUE or FALSE?

Cardiff, Swansea and Newport are cities in England.

10   When is Boxing Day?

    A   The day after Easter

    B   The day after Christmas Day

    C   The last Monday in August

    D   1 May

11   What age group does the National Citizen Service programme cover?

    A   All children up to the age of 17

    B   Pensioners

    C   16- and 17-year-olds

    D   18- to 30-year-olds

12   Which of the following statements is correct?

    A   Women in Britain make up about a quarter of the workforce.

    B   Women in Britain make up about half of the workforce.

13   What was the Beveridge Report of 1942 about?

    A   How to end the war in Europe

    B   How to treat the Germans and Japanese after the war

    C   Establishing a welfare state

    D   Overseas aid

14   Which of the following statements is correct?

    A   In a Crown Court case the judge decides the sentence when someone is found guilty.

    B   In a Crown Court case the jury decides the sentence when someone is found guilty.

15 Which UK city hosted the 2012 Paralympic Games?

    A   Belfast

    B   Cardiff

    C   Edinburgh

    D   London

16 Is the statement below TRUE or FALSE?

Britain and Germany developed Concorde, a passenger supersonic aircraft.

17 What is a fundamental principle of British life?

    A   A relaxed work ethic

    B   Democracy

    C   Extremism

    D   Religious faith

18 Is the statement below TRUE or FALSE?

The devolved Scottish government rules Scotland from Edinburgh.

19 Is the statement below TRUE or FALSE?

Catherine Howard was the sixth wife of Henry VIII.

20 What happened in 1215 to change the powers of the king?

    A   The Domesday Book

    B   Magna Carta

    C   The Reform Act

    D   The Black Death

21 Is the statement below TRUE or FALSE?

UK population growth has been faster in recent years.

22   Which of the following statements is correct?

     A   Local elections are normally held in May.

     B   Local elections are normally held in March.

23   Which TWO are famous British composers?

     A   Claude Debussy

     B   Johann Sebastian Bach

     C   Henry Purcell

     D   Ralph Vaughan Williams

24   Is the statement below TRUE or FALSE?

Life peers in the House of Lords can pass on their title to their first-born child.

Answers to Practice Test 1

	ANSWER	EXPLANATION
1	C	Halloween is celebrated on 31 October.
2	FALSE	The British constitution is not written down in any single document and therefore it is described as 'unwritten'.
3	A	Popular television programmes include regular soap operas such as *EastEnders* and *Coronation Street*.
4	D	Hereditary peers are members of the House of Lords who have inherited their titles. In 1999 they lost their automatic right to attend and now only a few are left.
5	TRUE	Pantomime plays are a British tradition. Many theatres produce a pantomime at Christmas time. They are based on fairy stories and are light-hearted plays with music and comedy.
6	C and D	The major political parties in the UK include the Conservative Party, the Labour Party and the Liberal Democrats.
7	C	Prime Minister's Questions takes place every week while Parliament is sitting.
8	A	The small claims procedure is an informal way of helping people to settle minor disputes without spending a lot of time and money using a lawyer.
9	A and B	Baptists and Methodists are Protestant Christian groups Other Protestant groups in the UK include the Church of England, the Church of Scotland, Presbyterians and Quakers.
10	B and D	Participation in community life and tolerance of those with different faiths and beliefs are

Answers to Practice Test 2

	ANSWER	EXPLANATION
1	C	In 1969, the voting age was reduced to 18 for men and women.
2	A and C	Easter and Christmas are two Christian festivals. Christmas celebrates the birth of Jesus Christ, and Easter marks his death on Good Friday and his rising from the dead on Easter Sunday.
3	A	Almost everybody in the UK who is in paid work must pay National Insurance Contributions. People who are self-employed must pay their own National Insurance Contributions.
4	C	Towns, cities and rural areas in the UK are governed by democratically elected councils, often called 'local authorities'. These are funded by money from central government and by local taxes.
5	A	Jane Austen and Charles Dickens are famous novelists. Jane Austen's books include *Pride and Prejudice* and *Sense and Sensibility.* Charles Dickens' novels include *Oliver Twist* and *Great Expectations.*
6	D	The 2010 coalition was formed by the Conservative and Liberal Democrat parties.

7	B	The UK is part of the United Nations (UN), an international organisation with more than 190 countries as members. The UN was set up after the Second World War and aims to prevent war and promote international peace and security.
8	A	The UK is governed by the parliament sitting in Westminster. Scotland, Wales and Northern Ireland also have parliaments or assemblies of their own, with devolved powers in defined areas.
9	FALSE	The Brit Awards is an annual event that gives awards to musicians in a range of categories, such as best British group and best British solo artist.
10	C	William of Normandy invaded England in 1066 and defeated Harold, the Saxon king of England, at the Battle of Hastings.
11	B	King Charles I believed that monarchs should be able to rule without approval from Parliament. This principle was one factor that led to the English Civil War in 1642.
12	B	Individual liberty is a fundamental principle of British life. British society is founded on fundamental values and principles, which all those living in the UK should respect and support.
13	A and C	Snowdonia is a national park in North Wales. Loch Lomond is in the Trossachs National Park in the west of Scotland.

14 FALSE   Members of the public are not allowed in Youth Courts, and the name or photographs of the accused young person cannot be published in newspapers or used by the media.

15 B   Elizabeth managed her relationship with Parliament skilfully. Her successor James I and his son Charles I were far less skilful in their handling of Parliament.

16 C   In 1605 a group of Catholics led by Guy Fawkes failed in their plan to kill the Protestant king with a bomb in the Houses of Parliament. The event is celebrated today as Bonfire Night.

17 B and C   Supporters of the king were known as Cavaliers and supporters of Parliament were known as Roundheads.

18 FALSE   The Restoration' refers to the re-establishment of the monarchy in 1660, when Charles II returned from exile after being invited back by Parliament.

19 A and C   Civil law is used to settle disputes between individuals or groups. Examples of civil law include housing law, employment law, consumer rights and laws related to the recovery of debt.

20 FALSE   The Scottish Parliament can pass laws for Scotland on all matters that are not specifically reserved to the UK Parliament.

21 B   Gilbert and Sullivan wrote comic operas, such as *HMS Pinafore*, *The Pirates of Penzance* and *The Mikado*.

22	B and C	Since 1997, some power has been devolved from central government. In 1999 the Scottish Parliament and the Welsh Assembly were established, to give people in Scotland and Wales more control over matters directly affecting them.
23	FALSE	The Union Flag comprises three crosses - the crosses of St George (England), St Andrew (Scotland) and St Patrick (Ireland).
24	TRUE	Allotments are plots of land that can be rented for growing fruit and vegetables.

Answers to Practice Test 3

	ANSWER	EXPLANATION
1	FALSE	People under 16 are not allowed to participate in the National Lottery.
2	B	King John was forced by his noblemen to agree to the Magna Carta, which restricted the power of the monarchy.
3	A and D	County Courts deal with a wide range of civil disputes, including divorce and other family matters, and breaches of contract.
4	A	The development of machinery transformed industries such as manufacturing and mining, and gave the UK industrial leadership from the early 18th century until the end of the 19th century.

5	C	The Tower of London was built by William the Conqueror after he became king in 1066.
6	B and C	The UK Parliament is formed by the House of Commons and the House of Lords.
7	B	Rowing is a popular sport in the UK, both as a leisure activity and as a competitive sport. There is a popular yearly race on the River Thames between Oxford and Cambridge Universities.
8	A and C	Among the many plays that Shakespeare wrote are *A Midsummer Night's Dream* and *Romeo and Juliet*.
9	FALSE	At the Battle of Trafalgar in 1805 Admiral Nelson defeated a combined French and Spanish fleet. He was killed during the battle.
10	A and B	The devolved administrations in Scotland, Wales and Northern Ireland can pass laws on matters that directly affect them, including health and education.
11	A	UK laws ensure people are not treated unfairly in any area of life or work because of their age, disability, sex, pregnancy and maternity, race, religion or belief, sexuality or marital status.
12	TRUE	By the Act for the Government of Wales during the reign of King Henry VIII, Wales united with England.
13	A and D	Roman Catholics and Baptists are Christian groups. Baptists are a Protestant Christian group. Other Protestant groups include the Church of England, Methodists, Presbyterians and Quakers.

14	B and D	There are responsibilities and freedoms which are shared by all those living in the UK. This includes freedom of speech and a right to a fair trial.
15	C	If an MP dies or resigns, there will be a fresh election, called a by-election, in his or her constituency.
16	B	Volunteering is working for good causes without payment. There are many activities you can do as a volunteer, such as working with the homeless and helping improve the environment.
17	A	Football is the UK's most popular sport. It has a long history in the UK and the first professional football clubs were formed in the late 19th century.
18	A	Charles II, whose father Charles I was executed at the end of the Civil War, was made king of Scotland by the Scots. He was forced into exile after being defeated by the English, but was restored to the throne of England in 1660 after the collapse of the republican Commonwealth.
19	A and B	People in the UK have to pay tax on their income, which includes profits from self-employment, and income from property, savings and dividends. Money raised from income tax pays for government services such as roads, education, police and the armed forces.
20	A	The Proms is an eight-week summer season of orchestral classical music. It has been organised by the British Broadcasting Corporation (BBC) since 1927.

21 B The Troubles' is a term used to describe the conflict that has occurred in Ireland between those who wish the North and South of Ireland to unite and those who wish the North to remain British.

22 B and D Admiral Lord Nelson commanded the British fleet at the Battle of Trafalgar in 1805. He died during the battle. The Duke of Wellington defeated Napoleon at the Battle of Waterloo in 1815.

23 TRUE Most people in the UK live in towns and cities but much of Britain is still countryside.

24 B To be able to vote in a parliamentary, local or European election, you must have your name on the electoral register. You can register by contacting your local council electoral registration office.

Answers to Practice Test 4

ANSWER EXPLANATION

1 B and C There are several British overseas territories in other parts of the world, such as the Falkland Islands and St Helena. They are linked to the UK but not part of it.

2 A If your driving licence is from a country in the European Union, Iceland, Liechtenstein or Norway, you can drive in the UK for as long as your licence is valid.

3	C and D	Sir Arthur Conan Doyle was a Scottish writer, best known for his stories about Sherlock Holmes. J K Rowling wrote the Harry Potter series of children's books.
4	A	The Whigs and Tories were the two main political groups in the 18th century. The Tories is a term that is still used today in regard to the Conservative Party.
5	B	The present voting age is 18, and was set in 1969.
6	B	Richard Arkwright developed more efficient textile factory production during the 18th century.
7	B and D	Almost everybody in the UK who is in paid employment, including self-employed people, must pay National Insurance Contributions. The money raised is used to pay for state benefits and services such as the state retirement pension and the National Health Service (NHS).
8	D	The vast number of people who died from the Black Death led to changes in the way society was structured. For example, new social classes appeared, including large landowners, and labour shortages meant that peasants demanded higher wages.
9	TRUE	1 April is known as April Fool's Day, when people play jokes on each other until midday.
10	B and C	Henry VIII is famous for breaking away from the Catholic Church of Rome and marrying six times.

11 B and C   The Premier League is the top league in English football and attracts a huge international audience. Many UK teams also compete in the UEFA (Union of European Football Associations) Champions League against other teams from Europe.

12 A   Magistrates are members of the local community. They usually work unpaid and do not need legal qualifications.

13 TRUE   Queen Anne had no surviving children, so Parliament decided to ask George of Hanover in Germany to become King George I of Great Britain.

14 C and D   Bonfire Night takes place on 5 November and people set off fireworks at home or in special displays. Remembrance Day is held on 11 November and commemorates those who died fighting for the UK and its allies.

15 FALSE   Florence Nightingale (1820-1910) was famous for her work to improve the quality of nursing and hospital conditions. She is often considered the founder of modern nursing.

16 TRUE   British society is founded on fundamental values and principles, which are based on history and traditions and are protected by law, customs and expectations.

17 C   Stonehenge is a famous Stone Age site in Wiltshire. It was probably built as a place for religious ceremonies.

18 C   St David is the patron saint of Wales, and St David's Day is celebrated on 1 March each year.

19 A and C — Criminal law relates to crimes that are usually investigated by the police or another authority such as a council, and which are punishable by the courts Such crimes include racial crimes and selling tobacco to anyone under the age of 18.

20 TRUE — The English language has many dialects and accents. In Wales many people speak Welsh. Gaelic is spoken in some parts of Scotland, and in Northern Ireland some people speak Irish Gaelic.

21 D — The National Assembly for Wales is based in Cardiff, the capital city of Wales.

22 C and D — Textile and engineering firms from the north of England and the Midlands sent agents to India and Pakistan to recruit workers.

23 A — Jane Austen was an English novelist who wrote many books, including *Sense and Sensibility* and *Pride and Prejudice*.

24 TRUE — The main political parties actively look for members of the public to join their debates, contribute to their costs, and help at elections.

Answers to Practice Test 5

ANSWER	EXPLANATION
1 A	Lancelot 'Capability' Brown and Gertrude Jekyll designed gardens around country houses.

2 C Elections for the European Parliament are held every five years. Elected members are called members of the European Parliament (MEPs).

3 B Scotland is a country of the UK, along with England, Wales and Northern Ireland.

4 TRUE Northern Ireland and Scotland have their own banknotes which are valid everywhere in the UK.

5 A In the UK, you must be at least 17 years old to drive a car or motor cycle and you must have a driving licence to drive on public roads.

6 D MPs are elected at a General Election, which is held at least every five years.

7 A and D After the 2010 General Election a coalition government was formed. The two parties in the coalition are the Conservatives and the Liberal Democrats.

8 A There was a clear policy in the 17th century to populate areas of Ireland with Protestants.

9 C *Beowulf* is an Anglo-Saxon poem, *The Tyger* is a poem by William Blake and *She Walks in Beauty* is a poem by Lord Byron.

10 A Sir Robert Walpole was the first person to use the term Prime Minister. He was Prime Minister from 1721 until 1742.

11 FALSE Snowdonia is a national park in North Wales. Its most well-known landmark is Snowdon, which is the highest mountain in Wales.

12 B Iron Age people spoke a Celtic-based language.

13	A and D	The Domesday Book is a record of the towns and villages in England. The Bayeux Tapestry tells the story of the Norman Conquest.
14	B	Father's Day occurs each year on the third Sunday of June. Children give cards or gifts to their fathers.
15	TRUE	Any man who forces a woman to have sex, including a woman's husband, can be charged with rape.
16	B	The Reformation occurred across Europe against the Roman Catholic Church, which led to the establishment of Protestant churches.
17	A	*The Mousetrap*, a murder-mystery play by Dame Agatha Christie, has been running in the West End since 1952.
18	FALSE	Everyone has the legal right to choose their religion, or to choose not to practise a religion.
19	D	Haggis is a traditional Scottish food. It is a sheep's stomach stuffed with offal, suet, onions and oatmeal.
20	FALSE	Isaac Newton was a famous scientist who developed our understanding of gravity.
21	B and D	The Scottish Grand National at Ayr, and Royal Ascot, a five-day meeting in Berkshire, are two important dates in the horse-racing calendar.
22	B	County Courts deal with a wide range of civil disputes. These include people trying to get back money that is owed to them, cases involving personal injury, family matters, breaches of contract, and divorce.

23	B and C	Australia and Canada are members of the Commonwealth. The Queen is the ceremonial head of the Commonwealth, which currently has 54 member states.
24	TRUE	In 2002 Winston Churchill (1874-1965), the British Prime Minister from 1940 until 1945, was voted the Greatest Briton of all time by the British public.

Answers to Practice Test 6

	ANSWER	EXPLANATION
1	B and D	Diwali is celebrated by Hindus and Sikhs. It celebrates the victory of good over evil and the gaining of knowledge.
2	A	The UK has a free press. This means that what is written in newspapers is free from government control.
3	FALSE	If an accused person is aged 10 to 17, the case is normally held in a Youth Court.
4	A	The Habeas Corpus Act was a major legal development ensuring that people could not be held prisoner without just cause.
5	C	The Channel Islands are closely linked with the UK but are not part of it, and have their own governments.
6	A	The Speaker of the House of Commons is an MP elected by fellow MPs in a secret ballot. The Speaker is neutral and does not represent a political party, even though he or she is an MP.

7	A	The Laurence Olivier Awards take place annually and awards are given in a variety of categories, including best director, best actor and best actress.
8	B and C	During the Middle Ages, English kings were involved in several Crusades in the Holy Land and took part in the Hundred Years War, which actually lasted 116 years.
9	FALSE	Dundee and Aberdeen are cities in Scotland.
10	B	Citizens of the UK, the Irish Republic or the Commonwealth must be aged 18 or over to stand for public office.
11	B	English settlers began to colonise the eastern coast of North America in the Elizabethan period.
12	B	Boudicca was a warrior queen who was queen of the Iceni in what is now eastern England. There is a statue of her near the Houses of Parliament in London.
13	FALSE	The jet engine and the radar were both developed in Britain in the 1930s.
14	B	Big Ben is the nickname of the great bell at the Houses of Parliament in London. Many people call the clock Big Ben as well.
15	B	Florence Nightingale treated soldiers who were fighting in the Crimean War. She later established the Nightingale Training School for nurses at St Thomas' Hospital in London.
16	D	All dogs in public places must wear a collar showing the name and address of the owner.

17	C	St Augustine and St Columba were early Christian missionaries who came to Britain to preach about Christianity. St Columba founded a monastery on the Isle of Iona. St Augustine spread Christianity in the south and became the first archbishop of Canterbury.
18	D	A jury has to listen to the evidence presented at the trial and then decide a verdict of 'guilty' or 'not guilty', based on what they have heard
19	A	Many sailing events are held throughout the UK, the most famous of which is at Cowes on the Isle of Wight.
20	TRUE	There are responsibilities and freedoms which are shared by all those living in the UK. These include respecting the rights of others, including their right to their own opinions.
21	A and D	There are laws to ensure that people are not treated unfairly in any area of work or life because of their disability, marital status, age, pregnancy and maternity, race, religion or belief, or sexuality.
22	A	The UK is a member of NATO (North Atlantic Treaty Organization!. NATO is a group of European and North American countries that have agreed to help each other if they come under attack.
23	B	The Industrial Revolution refers to the rapid development of factory-based production in Britain from the mid-18th century

24 A and B   Easter and Christmas are two Christian festivals
Christmas celebrates the birth of Jesus Christ,
and Easter marks his death on Good Friday
and his rising from the dead on Easter Sunday.

Answers to Practice Test 7

	ANSWER	EXPLANATION
1	D	The monarch opens the new parliamentary session each year. It is one of a number of important ceremonial roles.
2	TRUE	The period of the Enlightenment saw many new ideas emerge, including the principle that everyone should have the right to their own political and religious beliefs and that the state should not try to dictate to them.
3	FALSE	The UK has an ageing population. People in the UK are living longer than ever before.
4	A and D	The Commonwealth is based on the core values of democracy, good government and the rule of law.
5	B	Halloween is an ancient festival and has its roots in the pagan festival to mark the beginning of winter.

6	A and D	Isambard Kingdom Brunei (1806-59) was a famous engineer, and Florence Nightingale (1820-1910) established a training school for nurses, the first of its kind.
7	B	Great Britain' refers only to England, Scotland and Wales, not to Northern Ireland. The official name of the country is the United Kingdom of Great Britain and Northern Ireland.
8	TRUE	Forced marriage is where one or both parties do not or cannot give their consent to enter into the partnership. This is a criminal offence in the UK.
9	A	Football has a long history in the UK and the first professional football clubs were formed in the late 19th century.
10	B and C	The Reform Act of 1832 increased the number of men who could vote. It also abolished many parliamentary seats where there were few voters (called rotten boroughs), and increased the number of seats in the new cities and towns.
11	TRUE	Emmeline Pankhurst (1858-1928) was the leader of the women's suffrage movement that campaigned for women to be given the vote. Her supporters were called 'suffragettes'.
12	A and B	Sir Chris Hoy is a Scottish cyclist who has won six gold and one silver Olympic medals. Dame Kelly Holmes is a runner who has won two Olympic gold medals.
13	C	The Romans ruled Britain for almost 400 years, from AD 43 to AD 410.

14	A	MPs are elected through a system called 'first past the post'. This means that in each constituency, the candidate who gets the most votes is elected.
15	TRUE	Lent is a time when Christians take time to reflect and prepare for Easter. Traditionally, people would fast during this period and today many people will give something up, like a favourite food.
16	FALSE	The 'Swinging Sixties' refers to the 1960s. It was a period of rapid social change, including a growth in popular music and fashion. The Beatles and The Rolling Stones are associated with this period.
17	B and D	Famous UK festivals include Glastonbury and the Isle of Wight Festival. Festival season takes place across the UK every summer, with major events in various locations.
18	C	The Vikings first raided England in AD 789. They came from Denmark and Norway.
19	B	Sake Dean Mahomet (1759-1851) introduced both the curry house and the concept of shampooing to Britain.
20	A and B	There are many principles included in the European Convention on Human Rights, including prohibition of slavery and forced labour, and the freedom of thought, conscience and religion.
21	B	St Andrew is the patron saint of Scotland, and is celebrated on 30 November each year.

22 TRUE	There is no place for extremism or intolerance. British society is founded on fundamental values and principles which all those living in the UK respect and support.
23 A	The public can watch debates from public galleries in both the House of Commons and the House of Lords.
24 C and D	Political parties welcome new members. Members work hard to persuade people to vote for their candidates, for example, by handing out leaflets in the street or by knocking on people's doors and asking for their support (this is called 'canvassing').

Answers to Practice Test 8

ANSWER	EXPLANATION
1 D	Sir William Golding, Seamus Heaney and Harold Pinter have all won the Nobel Prize in Literature.
2 C	The public elect Police and Crime Commissioners (PCCs) in England and Wales. PCCs are responsible for the delivery of an efficient and effetive police force.
3 A	The Reform Act of 1832 also abolished pocket boroughs (constituencies controlled by one wealthy family) and rotten boroughs (constituencies which had hardly any voters). More parliamentary seats were given to town and cities.

4	A	Valentine's Day is on 14 February each year, when lovers exchange cards and gifts.
5	B and D	The Northern Ireland Assembly can make decisions on various issues, including agriculture and social services.
6	FALSE	In 1588 the English fleet defeated the Spanish Armada fleet, which had been sent to conquer England and restore Catholicism.
7	C	Oliver Cromwell was appointed Lord Protector after the execution of King Charles I, when England was a republic without a king.
8	FALSE	We shall fight them on the beaches' is a quote from a speech by Winston Churchill, the Prime Minister in 1940, about a potential German invasion.
9	C	The system of government in the UK is a parliamentary democracy. The UK is divided into parliamentary constituencies, and voters in each constituency elect a member of Parliament (MP) to represent them.
10	A	American colonies declared their independece from Britain in 1776. The War of Independence lasted until 1783, when the colonists defeated the British army and Britain recognised army and Britain recognised American independence.
11	D	If an MP dies or resigns, there will be a by-election in his or her constituency to elect a new MP.
12	A and B	The television and jet engine are two of many important inventions by Britons in the 20th century.

13 C   The Giant's Causeway is in Northern Ireland, on the north-east coast. It is a land formation of columns made from volcanic lava.

14 A   Almost everyone in paid work, including the self-employed, have to pay National Insurance Contributions (NICs). The contributions help pay for state benefits and services such as the state retirement pension and the National Health Service (NHS).

15 A   Civil servants are politically neutral, and are not political appointees.

16 TRUE   Mo Farah won gold medals in the 5,000 and 10,000 metres, and Jessica Ennis won a gold medal in the heptathlon.

17 C   There are age requirements in the UK regarding when you can drive different types of vehicles.

18 TRUE   Getting to know your neighbours can help you to become part of the community and make friends. Your neighbours are also a good source of help.

19 A   Sir Steve Redgrave is a famous rower who won gold medals in five consecutive Olympic Games.

20 A   The last successful invasion of England was in 1066 by William of Normandy.

21 A and B   St David, the patron saint of Wales, has a special day on 1 March. St Patrick, the patron saint of Northern Ireland (and the Republic of Ireland), has a special day on 17 March.

22 FALSE   John Constable was a famous British landscape painter.

23	A and C	The hovercraft was invented by Sir Christopher Cockerell and penicillin was discovered by Sir Alexander Fleming.
24	A	The UK offers citizens and permanent residents various freedoms and rights, including freedom of speech.

Answers to Practice Test 9

	ANSWER	EXPLANATION
1	TRUE	British society is founded on fundamental values and principles which all those living in the UK should respect and support. This includes participating in community life.
2	B	St Patrick, the patron saint of Northern Ireland (and the Republic of Ireland), has a special day on 17 March.
3	A	Drivers can use their driving licence up until the age of 70. After that, the licence is valid for three years at a time.
4	C and D	Popular English food include fish and chips, and roast beef which is served with potatoes, vegetables, Yorkshire puddings and other accompaniments.
5	B	Winston Churchill was the British Prime Minister from 1940 to 1945, during the Second World War.

6	D	If your car is over three years old, you must take it for a Ministry of Transport (MOT) test every year. If the vehicle is new, it will need an MOT test after three years, and then every year.
7	B	In the late 19th and early 20th centuries, an increasing number of women campaigned and demonstrated for women's rights, in particular the right to vote. They became known as 'suffragettes'.
8	B	Andy Murray is a Scottish tennis player and the first British man to win a singles tennis title in a Grand Slam tournament since 1936.
9	TRUE	All young people in the UK are sent a National Insurance number just before their 16th birthday. It ensures that the National Insurance Contributions and tax you pay are properly recorded against your name.
10	C and D	The Education Act of 1944 (also known as the Butler Education Act after the Minister of Education at the time. R A Butler) introduced free secondary education for all and established a clear division between the primary and secondary phases of education.
11	B	There are several British overseas territories in other parts of the world, such as the Falkland Islands.
12	A and B	In 1996 Ian Wilmot and Keith Campbell led a team that first succeeded in cloning a mammal. In the 1960s James Goodfellow invented the cash machine.

13	A	Members of the House of Lords are not elected by the people and do not represent a constituency.
14	B	The English were defeated at the Battle of Bannockburn by Robert the Bruce in 1314.
15	TRUE	Thomas Hardy (1840-1928) was a famous author and poet, whose best-known novels include *Far from the Madding Crowd* and *Jude the Obscure*.
16	A	George and Robert Stephenson were famous pioneers of early railway engines.
17	TRUE	The British Empire grew to cover India, Australia and large parts of Africa.
18	C and D	Edinburgh Castle is in Edinburgh, Scotland, and dates back to the Middle Ages. The London Eye is a Ferris wheel on the bank of the River Thames.
19	FALSE	Some powers have been devolved from central government to give people in Wales, Scotland and Northern Ireland more control over matters that directly affect them. Some policy and laws remain under central UK government control.
20	B and D	Recycle as much of your waste as you can, as this will reduce the amount of rubbish in landfill sites. Walking and using public transport creates less pollution than using a car.
21	A	National parks are areas of protected countryside that everyone can visit, and where people live, work and look after the landscape. There are 15 national parks in England, Wales and Scotland.

22	TRUE	In 1215 King John was forced by his noblemen to agree to the Magna Carta, which limited the powers of the monarchy.
23	B	The capital city of Wales is Cardiff.
24	B	A jury is made up of members of the public chosen at random from the electoral register.

Answers to Practice Test 10

	ANSWER	EXPLANATION
1	C	Isambard Kingdom Brunel was a famous Victorian engineer who built railway lines, bridges, tunnels and ships.
2	A and C	Solicitors are trained lawyers who give advice on legal matters. The Citizens Advice Bureau (CAB) can provide contact details of solicitors and the areas of law they specialise in.
3	A	The official home of the Prime Minister is 10 Downing Street in central London. The Prime Minister also has a country house called Chequers.
4	FALSE	Charles Dickens wrote a number of famous novels, including *Oliver Twist* and *Great Expectations*.
5	C	In Scotland a jury has 15 members. In England, Wales and Northern Ireland a jury has 12 members.

6 C — Mince pies are traditionally eaten at Christmas time. People also eat roast turkey and Christmas pudding.

7 A and C — UK-born and naturalised adult citizens, and citizens of the Commonwealth and Irish Republic who are resident in the UK, can vote in all UK elections. (Adult citizens of other EU states who are resident in the UK can vote in all elections except General Elections.

8 C — The National Trust in England, Wales and Northern Ireland, and the National Trust for Scotland, work to preserve important buildings, coastline and countryside.

9 A — The Prime Minister has the power to nominate peers for their own lifetime. These are called life peers. They are appointed by the monarch.

10 A and D — The Labour government that was elected in 1945 established the National Health Service (NHS) and a social security system for all.

11 B — Rugby originated in England in the early 19th century and is a popular sport in the UK today.

12 A and B — The UK belongs to many International bodies including NATO (North Atlantic Treaty Organization) and the Commonwealth.

13 B — The 1960s ('Swinging Sixties') are associated with rapid social change, with improved standards of living and the emergence of young people as a social force. This is reflected in the growth of fashion, music and cinema.

14 C — The £50 note is the highest-value note in circulation. Other denominations (values) of British notes are £5, £10 and £20.

15 TRUE   Being a school governor or school board member is a voluntary, unpaid activity. These roles play an important part in raising school standards.

16 B   The Reform Act of 1832 gave the vote to more men. Women did not achieve the right to vote until 1918.

17 B and C   Sissinghurst is in England and Bodnant Garden is in Wales.

18 A   The Queen is ceremonial head of the Commonwealth association of countries, which currently has 54 member states.

19 A   Henry VIII broke from the Catholic Church of Rome when it refused him a divorce. He established his own church that became the Church of England.

20 FALSE   William Blake, Lord Byron and Robert Browning were all 19th-century poets.

21 TRUE   The 1921 treaty led to Ireland being divided into two parts, Northern Ireland and the Irish Free State.

22 C and D   A number of social changes were introduced before the First World War, including the state retirement pension and free school meals.

23 A   Some cricket games can last for up to five days and still result in a draw.

24 FALSE   Britain fought a number of wars with France during the Middle Ages and later.

Answers to Practice Test 11

	ANSWER	EXPLANATION
1	A and D	Sir Francis Drake was a famous Elizabethan sailor who took part in the defeat of the Spanish Armada and also successfully sailed around the world.
2	B	Queen Elizabeth II has reigned since her father's death in 1952, and in 2012 she celebrated her Diamond Jubilee (60 years as queen).
3	B	The Good Friday Agreement of 1998 provided the basis for the establishment of the Northern Ireland Assembly.
4	D	Football is the UK's most popular sport. It has a long history in the UK, and the English Premier League attracts a huge international audience.
5	B	On becoming a UK citizen or permanent resident you will be agreeing to respect the laws, values and traditions of the UK.
6	TRUE	The daffodil is the national flower of Wales, and is worn on St David's Day.
7	C	The Chancellor of the Exchequer is responsible for the economy, and is a member of the cabinet.
8	C and D	The Dunkirk spirit' relates to the rescue of over 300,000 men from the beaches of Dunkirk in 1940. Many small boats, manned by volunteers, helped in the rescue.
9	D	The capital city of the UK is London, which is in England.

10 B — In the UK you can volunteer to donate your organs when you die, to help people in need of organ transplants.

11 C and D — Charles Dickens wrote many famous novels, including *Great Expectations* and *Oliver Twist*.

12 B — The Battle of Britain was fought in the air above Britain in 1940. The Germans needed to take control of the skies over Britain before they could attempt a seaborne invasion.

13 C — The king's supporters during the Civil War were called Cavaliers. Those who supported the Parliamentary cause were called Roundheads.

14 B — The Romans left England in AD 410 to defend other parts of their Empire. They had occupied England for 400 years.

15 A — Shopping locally for products will reduce your carbon footprint, because the products you buy will not have had to travel as far.

16 FALSE — An Ulster fry is a traditional food of Northern Ireland. It is a fried meal with bacon, eggs, sausage, black pudding, white pudding, tomatoes, mushrooms, soda bread and potato bread.

17 A — In the 19th century the UK produced more than half of the world's supplies of iron, coal and cotton cloth.

18 TRUE — Most citizens of the UK, the Irish Republic and the Commonwealth can stand for public office. There are some exceptions, including members of the armed forces.

19	B and D	Volunteering is working for good causes without payment. There are many benefits to volunteering, including meeting new people and making your community a better place.
20	FALSE	At the end of the Civil War, England became a republic and Oliver Cromwell was made Lord Protector.
21	B and D	David Hockney was an important contributor to the 'pop art' movement of the 1960s. Henry Moore is famous for his abstract sculptures.
22	FALSE	The age limit for jury service is 70. Anyone who is on the electoral register and is aged 18 to 70 can be asked to do jury service.
23	A	The Church of England is the official church of state in the UK. The monarch is head of the Church of England.
24	A and B	There are several different parts of government in the UK, which include the cabinet and the civil service.

Answers to Practice Test 12

	ANSWER	EXPLANATION
1	TRUE	The Chartists campaigned for reform of the voting system. The changes they wanted included annual elections and for all regions to be equal in the electoral system.
2	C and D	During the Great Depression of the 1930s many traditional heavy industries, such as shipbuilding, went into decline but new industries emerged and grew, such as aviation and the automobile industry.

3	A and B	You must be 17 or older to drive a motor cycle or car, and you must have a licence to drive on public roads.
4	A	The Bill of Rights of 1689 limited the powers of the king and increased the powers of Parliament.
5	B	The capital cities of the nations of the UK are: London (England), Cardiff (Wales), Edinburgh (Scotland) and Belfast (Northern Ireland).
6	TRUE	The term Great Britain dates from the union in 1707 of England and Scotland.
7	B and C	To apply to become a UK citizen or permanent resident, you must be able to speak and read English and have a good understanding of life in the UK.
8	A	King Alfred the Great united the Anglo-Saxon kingdoms of England and defeated the Vikings.
9	FALSE	There are some differences between the systems of courts in different parts of the UK.
10	FALSE	The BBC is financed by funds raised from TV licences. Everyone in the UK with a television, computer or other medium which can be used for watching TV must have a television licence.
11	B	MPs hold regular 'surgeries', where constituents can go in person to talk about issues that are of concern to them.
12	A	Hadrian's Wall was built on the orders of the Roman Emperor Hadrian to keep out the tribes who lived in what is today known as Scotland. Hadrian's Wall is now a UNESCO World Heritage Site.

13	B and C	In the 19th century, the medieval 'gothic' style became popular again. The Houses of Parliament and St Pancras Station were built at this time.
14	TRUE	Henry broke away from the Roman Catholic Church so he could divorce his wife Catherine of Aragon and marry Anne Boleyn. He married six times in total and had one son.
15	B and C	During the 1960s (a period known as the 'Swinging Sixties'), a number of social changes took place. Many social laws changed, for example, in regard to abortion and divorce.
16	C	The Church of Scotland is a Presbyterian Church, and it is Scotland's national Church.
17	FALSE	St Helena is a British overseas territory and not a Crown dependency.
18	C and D	Welsh cakes are a traditional Welsh snack made from flour dried fruits and spices. Haggis is a traditional Scottish food made from a sheep's stomach stuffed with offal, suet, onions and oatmeal.
19	A	Criminal laws related to crimes which are usually investigated by the police and punished by the courts.
20	A	Bobby Moore was the captain of the England football team that won the World Cup in 1966.
21	FALSE	Adult citizens of EU states (apart from the Republic of Ireland) who are resident in the UK can vote in all elections except General Elections.

22	B	The term 'suffragettes' relates to those who wanted women to gain legal rights and the right to vote in the late 19th and early 20th centuries.
23	B	There is no established Church in Wales or Northern Ireland. The official Church of state for the whole of the UK is the Church of England. Scotland also has a national Church, the Church of Scotland.
24	A	Country Courts are civil courts which deal with a wide range of civil disputes. These include disputes where people are trying to get back money that is owed to them.

Answers to Practice Test 13

	ANSWER	EXPLANATION
1	A and D	Britain has produced many great fashion designers, including Mary Quant and Vivienne Westwood.
2	B	The Tudor rose was a red rose with a white rose inside it, showing the alliance between the Houses of York and Lancaster, who had previously fought against each other.
3	B	The last Welsh rebellions were defeated by the middle of the 15th century.

4	B and C	If a judge finds that a public body is not respecting people's legal rights, they can order that the body changes its practices and/or pays compensation.
5	B	The phrase 'rain stopped play' is used in cricket. The phrase has now passed into everyday usage.
6	B	The Bayeux Tapestry commemorates the victory of William of Normandy at the Battle of Hastings in 1066.
7	TRUE	Shakespeare is regarded by many as the greatest playwright of all time.
8	A and D	In England, Wales and Northern Ireland, most minor criminal cases are dealt with in a Magistrates' Court. In Scotland, minor criminal offences go to a Justice of the Peace Court.
9	A	The rule of law is a fundamental principle of British life. British society is founded on fundamental values and principles which all those living in the UK should respect and support.
10	TRUE	Parliament eventually passed the Emancipation Act that abolished slavery in 1833. William Wilberforce played an important part in changing the law.
11	A and B	Alan Turing (1912-54) invented an early mathematical device that led to the development of the computer. Tim Berners-Lee (1955-) invented the World Wide Web.
12	C	The modern game of golf can be traced back to Scotland in the 15th century.

13	B	Police officers must obey the law They must not be rude or abusive, make a false statement, misuse their authority, or commit racial discrimination.
14	B	The UK National Anthem is called 'God Save the Queen' and is played at important national occasions and events attended by the Queen or the Royal Family.
15	TRUE	Everyone over 75 years of age can apply for a free television licence. Everyone in the UK with a television, computer or other medium which can be used for watching TV must have a television licence.
16	B and C	The Union Flag comprises the crosses of Saints George, Andrew and Patrick.
17	D	Many local authorities appoint a mayor, who is the ceremonial leader of the council (However in some towns, a mayor is elected to be the effective leader of the administration.)
18	B	Baptists, Methodists and Quakers are Protestant Christian groups.
19	FALSE	The Channel Islands are not a part of the UK but are closely linked to it. They have their own governments and are called 'Crown dependencies'.
20	B	D-Day refers to the allied invasion of Europe on 6 June 1944, which took place on the beaches of Normandy in France.
21	B	The capital city of Northern Ireland is Belfast.
22	A and B	The shamrock is the national flower of Northern Ireland, and the rose is the national flower of England.

23	A	There are a few members of Parliament (MPs) who do not represent any of the main political parties. They are called 'independents'.
24	FALSE	The Home Secretary is the government minister responsible for crime, policing and immigration

Answers to Practice Test 14

	ANSWER	**EXPLANATION**
1	B	Robert Burns is associated with Scotland. He was a poet. One of his best-known works is the song, *Auld Lang Syne*.
2	A and D	Britain was the first country to industrialise on a large scale. This happened because of the development of machinery and the use of steam power.
3	A	Several British writers have won the Nobel Prize in Literature, including Sir William Golding, Seamus Heaney and Harold Pinter.
4	A	School governors and school boards have an important part to play in raising school standards. This includes setting the strategic direction of the school.
5	B and C	After 1833, 2 million Indian and Chinese workers were employed to replace the freed slaves.

6 FALSE   In the UK many people enjoy a gamble on sports or other events. You have to be over 18 to go into a betting shop or a gambling club.

7 D   The Boer War took place in South Africa between the British army and the Boer settlers, who originally came from the Netherlands.

B B   By 1400 the preferred language of the English court was English, which was also the language of official documents.

9 A and C   Tilda Swinton and Colin Firth are two British film actors who have recently won Oscars.

10 A   The capital city of Scotland is Edinburgh.

11 D   In England, Wales and Northern Ireland, serious offences are tried in front of a judge and jury at a Crown Court. In Scotland, serious cases are heard in a Sheriff Court with either a sheriff Court with either a sheriff or a sheriff with a jury.

12 D   George Frederick Handel was born in Germany in 1695. He spent many years in the UK and became a British citizen in 1727.

13 B   Anyone on the electoral register aged between 18 and 70 can be asked to serve on a jury.

14 B   Proceedings in Parliament can be broadcast on television and reported in newspapers, and on the internet and radio.

15 TRUE   The Lake District is England's largest national park, covering 885 square miles (2, 292 square kilometres).

16	B	The Black Death in 1348 was a plague that killed over one third of the population. It was one of the worst disasters ever to strike Britain.
17	TRUE	Henry VIII had six wives and broke away from the Roman Catholic Church when the pope refused to grant him a divorce so he could marry again.
18	C	Since 1927 the BBC has sponsored and organised the annual Proms, an eight-week summer season of orchestral music.
19	A and C	The Grand National is held at Aintree near Liverpool, and Royal Ascot is a five-day race meeting held in Berkshire.
20	B	The monarch has regular meetings with the Prime Minister, and can advise, warn and encourage, but the decisions on government policies are made by the Prime Minister and cabinet.
21	TRUE	Like the Channel Islands, the Isle of Man is a Crown dependency with its own government.
22	C	In July 1916 the British suffered 60,000 casualties on the first day of the Battle of the Somme.
23	TRUE	Pressure groups are organisations which try to influence government policy. They play an important role in politics and the democratic process.
24	A and C	Sir Alfred Hitchcock and Ridley Scott are British film directors who have had great success in the UK and internationally.

Answers to Practice Test 15

	ANSWER	EXPLANATION
1	D	The Huguenots were French Protestants who faced persecution in France so they escaped and came to England to live.
2	A and B	The television was developed by John Logie Baird in the 1920s. Tim Berners-Lee invented the World Wide Web in 1990.
3	C	Many theatres produce a pantomime at Christmas time. They are light-hearted plays with music and comedy, enjoyed by family audience.
4	B	Civil servants in the UK are politically neutral, and are not political appointees.
5	TRUE	Civil law cases relate to disputes between individuals or groups.
6	B and C	Ellie Simmonds won gold medals for swimming at the 2008 and 2012 Paralympic Games. Baroness Tanni Grey-Thompson has won 16 Paralympic medals for athletics.
7	C	The Speaker is chosen by other members of Parliament (MPs) in a secret ballot. The Speaker's role is to chair debates in the House of Commons.
B	TRUE	Margaret Thatcher won her first General Election in 1979 and was re-elected in 1983 and 1987. She left office in 1990.

9	A	The public in England and Wales elect Police and Crime Commissioners (PCCs). The first elections for PCCs were held in November 2012.
10	B	The BBC is a British public service broadcaster providing television and radio programmes. It is the only wholly state-funded media organisation that is independent of government.
11	B and C	In the UK Mothering Sunday is celebrated on the Sunday three weeks before Easter and Father's Day on the third Sunday in June. Children send cards and give gifts on these days.
12	A	Entrance is free to watch debates at the Houses of Parliament. You can get a ticket from your local MP or queue on the day.
13	A and B	There are responsibilities and freedoms which are shared by all those living in the UK. These include respecting and obeying the law, and treating others with fairness.
14	C	When Adolf Hitler invaded Poland in 1939, Britain, alongside France, declared war on Germany to stop his aggression.
15	A	The Wars of the Roses lasted from 1455 until 1485. It was a civil war between supporters of the House of York and supporters of the House of Lancaster.
16	FALSE	Most people in the UK live in towns and cities, but much of Britain is still countryside.
17	C	Dylan Thomas (1914-1953) was a Welsh poet and writers. One of his famous works is *Under Milk Wood*.

18	B	People under the age of 16 are not allowed to participate in the National Lottery.
19	A	You have to pass both a theory and a practical driving test before you are given a full driving licence.
20	A	James VI of Scotland was a cousin of Queen Elizabeth. When she died without leaving an heir. James also became King James I of England.
21	TRUE	You can see the Crown Jewels at the Tower of London. The Tower of London was first built by William the Conqueror after he became king in 1066.
22	A and C	William Wilberforce played an important role in ending slavery, which was eventually abolished in the British Empire in 1833. The Quakers set up the first anti-slavery groups in the late 1700s.
23	B	England, Scotland, Wales and Northern Ireland make up the UK.
24	A	Getting into debt is a civil matter, dealt with by a Country Court or the small claims procedure.

Answers to Practice Test 16

	ANSWER	EXPLANATION
1	FALSE	During the Great Depression of the 1930s, parts of the UK suffered mass unemployment.

2	B	The Chancellor of the Exchequer is the cabinet minister responsible for the economy.
3	C	Australia, Canada and South Africa remained a part of the British Empire and joined the Commonwealth.
4	C	You must be aged 18 or over to buy alcohol (people under 18 may be able to drink alcohol in pubs or restaurants if they are with someone over 18).
5	FALSE	The Wimbledon Championships are associated with tennis.
6	C and D	Many of the great thinkers of the Enlightenment were Scottish. Adam Smith developed ideas about economics. David Hume wrote about human nature.
7	D	Lewis Hamilton, Jensen Button and Damon Hill are all British winners of the Formula 1 World Championship.
8	C	When an MP dies or resigns, a by-election is held. This is an election held in that constituency to elect a new MP.
9	A	Plymouth, Norwich and Leeds are cities in England.
10	FALSE	The House of Lords is normally more independent of government than the House of Commons.
11	A and B	Thomas Hardy was an author and poet, whose novels include *Far from the Madding Crowd* and *Jude the Obscure*. Graham Greene wrote many novels including *The Heart of the Matter*, *The Honorary Consul*, *Brighton Rock* and *Our Man in Havana*.

12	C	In 1066, William of Normandy invaded England and defeated King Harold at the Battle of Hastings.
13	A and C	William Shakespeare (1564-1616) wrote many famous plays and poems. Many of his works are still performed today.
14	A	The National Trust in England, Wales and Northern Ireland, and the National Trust for Scotland, work to preserve important buildings, coastline and countryside.
15	C	There are responsibilities and freedoms which are shared by all those living in the UK. These include looking after yourself and your family.
16	FALSE	General Elections in the UK are held at least every five years.
17	C	Margaret Thatcher became Britain's first woman Prime Minister in 1979 and won the next two elections in 1983 and 1987. She resigned as Prime Minister in 1990.
18	B and C	The Beatles and The Rolling Stones, both formed in the 1960s, continue to have an influence on music in the UK and abroad.
19	B	Northern Ireland has a system called 'individual registration', which means all those entitled to vote must complete their own registration form.
20	A	There are public holidays each year, called bank holidays, when banks and many other businesses close for the day.
21	A	The Highland Clearances took place in Scotland when crofters were forced off their land to make way for sheep and cattle grazing.

22	B	Pool is a traditional pub game, along with darts. Pub quizzes are also popular. Most communities have a local pub that is a natural focal point for social activities.
23	B	Henry VIII needed the Pope's agreement to a divorce. When this was refused, he established the Church of England with himself in charge.
24	FALSE	On average, girls leave school with better qualifications than boys. Also, more women than men study at university.

Answers to Practice Test 17

	ANSWER	EXPLANATION
1	C	The Roman Emperor Hadrian built the wall in the north of England to keep out the Picts (ancestors of the Scottish people).
2	A	'To be or not to be' is a quotation from *Hamlet*, written by William Shakespeare.
3	A and B	During the 18th century, new ideas about politics, science and philosophy developed. This period became known as 'the Enlightenment'.
4	A	The monarch is head of state of the UK, and all Acts of Parliament are made in the monarch's name.
5	D	Sir Edwin Lutyens was a famous 20th-century architect who designed the Cenotaph in Whitehall.

6	TRUE	The ending of the First World War on 11 November 1918 is still commemorated to this day.
7	B and D	A civil war known as the Wars of the Roses broke out in 1455 between supporters of the House of Lancaster and the House of York. It ended in 1485 at the Battle of Bosworth, when King Richard III of the House of York was killed.
8	D	Some powers have been devolved from central government to give people in Wales, Scotland and Northern Ireland more control over matters that directly affect them.
9	FALSE	Cardiff, Swansea and Newport are all cities in Wales.
10	B	Boxing Day is the day after Christmas Day and is a bank holiday.
11	C	The National Citizen Service programme is aimed at 16- and 17-year-olds. It gives them the opportunity to enjoy outdoor activities, develop their skills and take part in a community project.
12	B	Women in Britain make up about half of the workforce. Employment opportunities for women are much greater than they were in the past.
13	C	The Beveridge Report of 1942, called *Social Insurance and Allied Services*, set out ideas on how to fight the five evils of Want, Disease, Ignorance, Squalor and Idleness.
14	A	In a Crown Court a judge decides the sentence when someone is found guilty.
15	D	London hosted the 2012 Paralympic Games.

16	FALSE	Concorde was a joint development with France, not Germany.
17	B	Democracy is a fundamental principle of British life. British society is founded on fundamental values and principles which all those living in the UK should respect and support.
18	TRUE	The Scottish Parliament sits in Edinburgh, the capital city of Scotland.
19	FALSE	Catherine Howard, a cousin of Henry VIII's second wife, Anne Boleyn, was Henry's fifth wife.
20	B	The Magna Carta was a charter drawn up by King John's noblemen. It laid down basic rights that still prevail today.
21	TRUE	UK population growth has been faster in recent years, due to migration into the UK and longer life expectancy.
22	A	For most local authorities, local elections for councillors are held in May every year.
23	C and D	Henry Purcell wrote church music, opera and other pieces, and developed a distinctive British style. Ralph Vaughan Williams was strongly influenced by traditional English folk music.
24	FALSE	Most members of the House of Lords are now life peers, who are nominated by the Prime Minister to sit in the House of Lords for their own lifetime.

**LIVE IN THE UK**
.co.uk

You can access 100s of free test questions on our website liveintheuk.co.uk. You will also find our 2022 British citizenship course which covers all of the content and what you need to learn in order to pass the Life in the UK test.

Printed in Great Britain
by Amazon

86097086R00075